Investigating THE CASE OF THE
DROWNING MEN
The Smiley Face Serial Murder Theory

Investigating THE CASE OF THE
DROWNING MEN
The Smiley Face Serial Murder Theory

Written and illustrated by EPONYMOUS ROX © 2012
Special Black & White Illustrated Discount Edition
ISBN 10: 1477668411 - ISBN 13: 978-1477668412

The subject matter of this investigation is derived from a variety of public records and databases including police and forensic reports. It may therefore contain themes and content not suitable for all audiences. The drown cases featured herein were originally classified by law enforcement agencies as accidents and, although a few have since been reclassified as 'undetermined' or as homicides, all of them, per the date of this publication, remain unsolved and inactive. However, a number of victims' families are soliciting support from the public to overturn prior 'accidental' rulings so the deaths can be reinvestigated as murders, and are even offering substantial rewards for any information that will lead to the arrest and conviction of the party or parties responsible. Wherever available, active links to websites and other reading material for further study of specific victim profiles have been provided at the conclusion of each relevant chapter as well as in the comprehensive resource index at the end of this publication. The views and opinions expressed in THE CASE OF THE DROWNING MEN are based on private, independent research and consultations. As such, the findings and conclusions contained in it are considered speculative in nature and do not necessarily reflect the views and opinions of the publisher, the individuals or agencies who have been quoted, or the author. Some data/sources limited via fair usage percents are only extracts.

This book is dedicated to all who have died in vain or too young. May you find, and rest in, peace.

"Justice delayed is justice denied."

William Gladstone (1809 - 1898)

CONTENTS

Chapter 1: Dead Certain

Since the mid 1990's, in the northernmost district of America where Interstates 90 and 94 merge to cut a scenic route toward the west, crossing nearly a dozen states along the way and skirting the border with Canada, scores of young men are vanishing every year without a trace. Only to turn up days, weeks, or months later in nearby bodies of water, dead.

Occurring mainly between the months of September to April, it's the same story repeating itself every time, with little variation: A young man goes out for the evening with his friends, gets separated from them some time after midnight, and, despite massive search efforts by his loved ones to find out what became of him, is never seen alive again.

For local law enforcement officials the hunt for lost men over the past fifteen years has become an all too familiar tale of woe as well, not the least because it's costly and disruptive. But as far as police are concerned, even before they launch an investigation, even before a body's been recovered from the water and an autopsy performed, it's always a cut-and-dry case: "No signs of foul play."

Young people are simply drinking too much, the authorities claim. Young people will do crazy and stupid things when they're inebriated. They'll even throw themselves into an icy river or lake and drown.

Seems a reasonable enough explanation on its face, if only one or two fatalities occurring every once in awhile, and a scenario that's not totally impossible to imagine either. But by the hundreds?

And why only males then? All matching the same description? Washing up in places thoroughly searched before…?

I first stumbled upon the case of the drowning men in early 2012, and quite by accident. Indeed, whatever it was I'd originally been researching at the moment, it was undoubtedly not related to death or dying, and I'm also positive it had nothing to do with H_2O and its cold-weather hazards. But the brain is an efficient machine and though its focus may be directed to one particular matter it's still constantly processing everything else on the periphery; sorting, analyzing and connecting all the data-bytes it comes across. Like pieces of a jigsaw puzzle. Like dots on a map.

Scientists say one of the things the human brain is very quick to detect is a pattern. If so, that must be the reason why, when I glanced at the February article concerning yet another youth who had wandered away from his buddies and whose corpse was found shortly thereafter floating in the Mississippi, I blurted aloud, "What, not again," and clicked on the news link. Before that day, before I began to consciously pay attention to this issue, I can honestly say I'd never known of anyone, young or old, male or female, to drink and drown in autumn, winter or spring. Not in all the time I've lived in this, the affected area.

Like my fellow citizens who are also lifelong residents of the Great Lakes region—growing up here, going to school, working, vacationing, socializing—I can attest that these two things, drinking and drowning in cold weather, have never been synonymous with each other. Drowning after a night out on the town with your friends during the chilly months of September through April, with nobody else around to help, with no witnesses, just isn't as inevitable as the police would have us all suddenly believe it is. It's not, regardless of what age you are or your close proximity to the water, an ordinary way to perish.

This is probably because in these parts, even when people are drunk out of their minds, they don't usually drown outdoors unless they're in the act of swimming, or else involved in some other form of water recreation like waterskiing or boating. Activities which, because of our cold, northern climate, are only safely executed in rivers, lakes and ponds approximately three months out of the calendar year, in June, July, and August.

The rest of the time the water's simply too cold to go in, and most everybody (native and transplant alike) understands that if water is at or below 65 degrees Fahrenheit, it's not only brutally uncomfortable, it can kill you—a body cools in water twice as fast as it does in air, losing an approximate rate of five degrees per hour. Death from hypothermia only takes about three hours in 40 to 60 degree water; less than two hours at 35 to 40 degrees; and less than three-quarters of an hour at temperatures below 35 degrees.

Those deadly equations are fairly easy to master and, in the land of lakes and rivers and ponds and streams and brooks, youngsters are taught them early on. As for the rare and reckless few who fail to grasp the math, to be perfectly candid, they don't usually make it to their early teens, let alone full adulthood.

The average age of the males who go missing and are later found drowned in the Interstate 90 and 94 Corridor is between 19 and 23 years. In the entire grouping perhaps a handful have been only 17 and a few others as old as 30, although it must be said, in the case of the more mature victims, they didn't look anywhere near their true age in posters or photographs.

Grown men drowning in cold weather on their way home at night. That's become a strange new fact of life and the weird new math those who reside in the northern corridor have now had to learn, based upon figures which have been accumulating for nearly the past two decades.

We're fond of and rely on facts and numbers to inform us here in the northland because, overall, we're an educated people. Our extensive waterways, highways, railways, large cities, major industries and fertile farmlands have contributed to make the region one of the most affluent in the country. As a result, many of the world's finest universities can be found in this region as well, and an overwhelming majority of us have attended them. We're a schooled and highly trained bunch of skeptics we are, and even a bit conservative leaning.

Which is to say, we tend to mull things over long before we act. We don't jump to conclusions…

In 2004 the April drowning of yet another popular, athletic, and bright 21-year-old male of medium build, at the University of Wisconsin in La Crosse, provided the tipping point for that community's stoical tolerance of the matter. In terms of these events La Crosse is one of the hotspots, and by that year there'd been way too many of the same type of men dying under identical circumstances for the public to view it anymore as coincidence. With the inexplicable disappearance of honor student Jared Dion the city was up in arms, and when his body was eventually discovered downriver, the once-whispered suspicions of murder instantly morphed into full blown allegations of a serial killer or a gang of serial killers stalking college-age men in the area, not to mention accusations of police involvement and a cover up.

There were roughly 51,000 people living in La Crosse in 2004, according to the U.S. Census, and, to be sure, they weren't all hapless students; city officials and the police department were late to acknowledge a crisis at hand, and, when they did finally react to it, the town-hall meetings they commandeered to dismiss the public's fears as unfounded did little or nothing to calm things down again. Every public debate concerning the river deaths was jam-packed and rapidly descended into a shouting match.

It was probably in a last ditch effort to restore the peace as well as to mitigate harm to the university's reputation that an open letter from faculty members at the University of Wisconsin in La Crosse was penned and then distributed to the student body. Co-authored by the Chairs of the Psychology and Sociology departments and titled *Why we are 99.9% sure it is NOT a serial killer - a data based explanation*, this urgent communiqué implored students to use their "critical thinking skills" to evaluate what was really going on in their town. A levelheaded analysis would prove these were only drownings, not murders, the professors assured them. A string of terribly tragic and utterly preventable accidents:

1. Students are drinking too much and incapacitating themselves, a condition which drives some to seek out the river to refresh themselves, during which they slip and fall in.

2. Only men are drowning as a result of intoxication because women are more savvy these days and don't wander around alone at night, especially not if they've been partying.

3. Annually, almost ten times as many males die during water recreational activities and in other types of accidents than females do. Alcohol plays a role in a number of these cases.

4. There are no drowning deaths at nearby universities like Madison because their campuses are beside lakes. Whereas La Crosse's campus is situated right on the river's edge, and rivers, being suddenly deep and fast flowing, are far more dangerous.

5. The similarities between the victims constitute "illusory correlations" which can readily be explained through other qualifying factors.

Stepping into the middle of a community's fray and trying to mediate it was highly unusual for a university, and, in light of the dire subject matter of their "data based explanation" and the negative impact advertising it might have had on future enrollment, a rather risky PR move, too. But the professors' treatise was also an intelligent, compassionate, and methodical approach to debunking the serial murderer theory before it could take root—the first of many—so the gamble was well worth it. Moreover, this strategy appears to have been quite successful. At least for awhile.

But in 2005, 2006 and 2007, drunk *and sober* young men continued to go missing along the interstates, sometimes two or more in the very same time span. Their corpses eventually to be retrieved from such rivers as the Calumet, the Hudson, the Charles, the Mississippi, the Milwaukee, the Wabash and the Wisconsin, as well as a number of area lakes, including Great Lake Michigan, Lake LaVerne, and the University at Madison's nearby Lake Mendota. These latter deaths occurring in seeming defiance of the UW-L professors' sweeping assertion that a lake doesn't pose the same risk for drowning because "it becomes gradually deeper and is not moving swiftly."

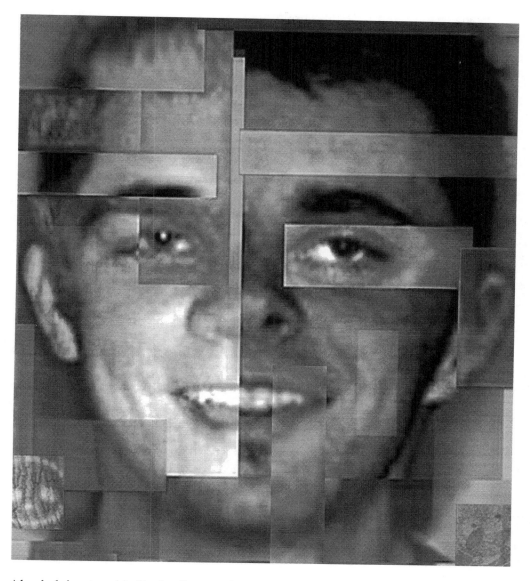

Also helping to rekindle the flames of conflict between believers and nonbelievers of a serial killer, new information had begun trickling in from reliable outside investigators which suggested that dozens of the questionable drownings could be linked now not only by an identifiable victimology and a distinct manner of death, but also through cryptic symbols like smiley faces and other taunting messages left at the scenes of a some of the suspected murders.

A subsequent inspection throughout the region confirmed that there was in fact sinister-looking graffiti of this sort at many a river's edge or lakefront, and, as with the ruckus at La Crosse Wisconsin just a few years prior, a large percent of the student populations in these locations, together with their families and the local citizenry, became understandably very worked up about these findings. Terrified.

It was investigative reporter Kristi Piehl from KSTP-TV out of Minnesota who first broke the story in 2008 of serial killers drowning men along Interstate 90 and 94, and of the doggedly determined pair of retired NYPD detectives in hot pursuit of them. The segment ultimately earning her an Emmy but apparently costing her a job. From that special report, the concept of a "Smiley Face Killer Gang" was born and went instantly viral, not just on websites and in chatrooms, but also in the major media outlets.

ABC, MSNBC, CNN and the Associated Press, among others, picked up the local news item and carried it nationwide, in so doing, widely broadcasting the seeds of what would become one of the most hotly-contested conspiracy theories of our time.

Once again, pandemonium broke out as anxious citizens began mobilizing and actively trying to bypass their own police departments' authority, demanding instead that federal assistance be provided in order to apprehend a fiendish network of elusive serial murderers stalking, abducting and drowning specific types of young males across the northland.

Experts in criminology and forensic pathology studied the various case profiles as well, and, noting the telltale spikes in certain localities, they also began expressing similar opinions.

"The probability is virtually zero that five intoxicated students just happened to walk similar or even different routes and end up on the riverbank." *Dr. Maurice Godwin, criminal investigative psychologist, commenting on the La Crosse Wisconsin cluster*

"They could have been murdered but the person was just so good at doing it that they didn't leave any physical evidence…[they] could sedate and drown him in a tub or something like that and then throw him in the river." *John Kelly, psychotherapist and profiler*

"The statistics are so stacked against this number of men, young men, Caucasian males, found in bodies of water in that cluster of states, within that period of time." *Dr. Cyril Wecht, forensic pathologist*

"If you actually look at the statistics on drownings, most drownings occur during the summer and they're related to water activities like boating and water skiing and things like that. Very few drownings actually occur during the winter." *Lee Gilbertson, Professor of Criminal Justice at St. Cloud University*

The supporting evidence for those conclusions was so compelling, in fact, that two high-level state representatives joined in the furor. Senator Sensenbrenner from Wisconsin and U.S. Congressman McNulty from New York both submitted requests directly to the FBI urging the Bureau to formally investigate the serial murders being perpetrated in their states and to take swift actions to end them.

"Yes, there's a serial murderer—alcohol," La Crosse's flustered chief of police, Edward Kondracki, retorted when confronted with these latest developments. But, "a rogue cop…or national smiley face gang…there is no serial killer!"

In this growing war of words, rival local-news networks who had failed to show any real interest in the story before felt obliged now to weigh in, some seeking to ridicule the award-winning reporter who had intrepidly launched the Smiley Face Murder Theory into the national spotlight.

Veteran columnist Steve Perry from the *Minnesota Monitor* unabashedly said of her, "Let the record show that Kristi Piehl of KSTP has done her part to bring the yarn to the huddled masses yearning to breathe the vapors of another massive conspiracy." And reporter Brian Lambert at *Minneapolis St.Paul Magazine* angrily proclaimed that a story depicting serial drownings as actual serial slayings in disguise going on to earn a coveted journalism award was "ludicrous," and that the very idea of a serial murderer being responsible for the spate of area deaths, "boggles every rational instinct."

But because a homegrown rumor, many years in the creation, had suddenly spiraled into a legend overnight, it would now require much more than scorn and carefully constructed editorial pieces to slam the lid back on the can of worms it had opened. The American public's imagination and its keen interest in the case had been ignited, and it would take a multi-pronged effort to fully squelch the serial killer theory this time. In that process, a number of reputations would necessarily have to be sullied, a few investigations closed, and taxpayers' monies liberally spent in order to increase security, and a sense of security, in communities close to water.

Fences, river patrols, safe buses, surveillance cameras, targeted campaigns of every variety aimed at damage control— these costly measures could be justified because public officials knew that, to govern properly, people couldn't be living in fear day and night, and they couldn't be distrustful of their law enforcement officers, either. Most importantly, university towns couldn't expect students to continue flocking to them in droves, as many in this region have been accustomed to for over a century, if they're suddenly afraid they'll end up victims of violent crimes there. When it comes to social strife and chaos, in the end *the end* always does justify the means employed, and, as can be seen today, these strenuous attempts to solve "the problem" have been effective in crushing the ugly stories and criticisms that were running rampart not so long ago.

All throughout the northern corridor now, a truce appears to be in place and holding, and, for the most part, it's been pretty quiet these past couple of years.

But then there is that plaguing issue of a steadily rising body count.

Chapter 2: Anatomy of a Drowning

For those who think that drowning is a pleasant way to go, think again. Drowning is a violent assault on the body during which the frightened victim fiercely, albeit briefly, battles to survive. Death follows exhaustion within only two or three minutes.

Technically, it is true that a person can drown in as little as a cup of water. A cup, a puddle, a ditch, a bathtub—anytime liquid enters the air passages and lungs, even if someone doesn't die immediately, it can still turn fatal because there are a host of medical complications which arise that are always life-threatening, such as pneumonia and renal failure. These type of delayed fatalities are known as "secondary drownings" and, although their symptoms may develop over the course of several days, or even longer for some patients, they're usually triggered within only a few hours of the initial incident.

But most victims drown fully submerged in water when the nose and mouth inadvertently become covered. Sometimes, when there is an instantaneous glottal spasm blocking off oxygen, or a preexisting medical condition, death can be automatic without any signs of a struggle. In the majority of drownings, however, this is not the case. Struggling is one of the key stages leading to unconsciousness and death. In fact, so intense can this final fight for life be that, in more than ten percent of drowning fatalities, an autopsy will actually reveal bruised and ruptured muscles, particularly in the shoulders, chest and neck. Evidence of injuries of this nature suggest to a medical examiner the strong likelihood that a victim was alive in the water at the time of their demise and not placed there already dead.

The stages of a full-immersion drowning event are fairly quick and, because the victim's airways are being blocked, either by water and/or the epiglottis, it's often completely soundless. There will be panicked thrashing as the victim desperately attempts to get air and to grab onto nearby objects for security, and then, when they can no longer hold their breath, they'll begin to inhale water in large quantities, gulping it into their stomach as well. This action also rapidly circulates water throughout their other systems and bloodstream with differing biochemical reactions depending on whether they're in saltwater or in fresh. This last stage of drowning ends with coughing, vomiting, convulsions, loss of consciousness, death, and rigormortis.

Very shortly after the victim dies their body will start to sink. If retrieved soon thereafter, their arms and hands may display cadaveric spasm, a posture in death borne out of extreme mental anguish and which reveals the person's final thoughts and movements as they frantically fought to stay alive.

If a victim is not promptly retrieved at death, then, without exception and no matter how deep or how swift the water may be, their corpse will continue to drift downward until it reaches the bottom. This is where it will remain in a somewhat fetal position until gases from putrefaction cause it to rise to the surface once more.

A semi-fetal posture is the norm for all drown victims, so if divers do locate such a body before it ascends, but it isn't in this pose and/or the head is seen to be tilted to one side, they must include these observations in their police recovery report, as it reveals the victim died on land and was put in the water post-rigormortis.

Typically, once the body does emerge on its own, it will surface in the general vicinity of where the victim originally went under. From this location the water may then carry the corpse along for quite a distance, depending on the strength of the currents or if it becomes ensnared and is thereby prevented.

Refloat largely varies on the water's depth and temperature, taking only a matter of hours to occur if extremely warm and up to two weeks or longer if at 40 degrees Fahrenheit or less. The timetable, therefore, is not fixed but is loosely as follows: at 40 degrees Fahrenheit it takes approximately fourteen to twenty days for a drown victim's corpse to resurface; at 50 degrees ten to fourteen days; at 60 degrees seven to ten days; at 70 degrees three to seven days; and at 80+ degrees one to two days or sooner. In very cold and very deep bodies of water, like certain oceans or the Great Lakes of North America, it's not unusual at all for a drown victim to never resurface, lying on the bottom in a state of suspended decomposition until their body eventually disintegrates or is otherwise destroyed.

But in temperate oceans, rivers, lakes, ponds, pools, reservoirs, quarries, or the like, a corpse will inevitably rise again, sooner or later, occasionally exploding to the surface if it was deliberately anchored. And when it does reappear, if the person did genuinely die from drowning, then they will always be discovered floating face down in the water, with the head drooping forward and lower than the rest of the body.

Lividity, the pooling of blood and fluids, will then have permanently settled into the under regions of the corpse by then, weighting it from beneath and essentially acting as a ballast so that, even when disturbed, say by a collision with a boat, it will return to this original position.

If one can stomach a physical inspection of the body and knows what to look for, at this point it becomes relatively easy to determine the length of time a victim's actually been submerged. However, because a previously sunken body could have been slowly dragged along the water's bed by currents and thereby further damaged against rocks and similar objects, or even partially eaten by marine animals, it may be difficult for the layperson to ascertain if any visible injuries happened in life or were obtained postmortem.

Damaged or not, though, if a body has been in the water for at least one to 48 hours, wrinkling of the skin will be present already, particularly on the palms of the hands and fingertips and on the soles and toes of the feet. Noticeable blanching and bloating of the epidermis may also be underway too, with pronounced blotches and discolorations ranging in hue from pink to dark red distributed unevenly across the body.

In excess of the above time period, the victim's epidermis may look a greenish bronze and will have begun pimpling and even pre-peeling as fat deposits just beneath it slowly transform into a soapy material and loosen the skin. This is especially true of the flesh on the hands and feet which will slip off on their own—or when tugged on—just like gloves, a process of decay aptly named "degloving". If signs of degloving are already evident on such a corpse, special care must be taken in recovering the body from the water, as additional harm can easily be inflicted when physically grappling with it or maneuvering it about with hooks and mechanical devices.

Once it has been successfully recovered, a waterlogged body will rapidly deteriorate when fully exposed to air, therefore an autopsy must be performed immediately in order to help determine the exact cause of death and the manner. This may seem superfluous, but the fact is death by drowning is not wholly assumed by medical experts and law enforcement, especially where there have been no witnesses to unequivocally substantiate it.

In forensic terms, there is nothing whatsoever deemed "classic" about any drowning, no one particular physical characteristic manifesting in a corpse that would aid in expediting such a ruling. Because of this, the methodology for reaching a determination that it was a water death and accidental is one that is chiefly focused on excluding foul play. This places a great deal of importance on the initial investigative role of police personnel who could inform or misinform a medical examiner with their onsite reports and early conclusions.

Even the autopsy is insufficient on its own for definitively pinpointing the victim's cause of death as an accidental drowning, but the line of inquiry a medical examiner follows during this phase of the inquest is to review the circumstances of how the deceased person reportedly first entered the water and to try to judge if the body they're viewing matches up to that version of events. If so, and the death indeed appears benign, the medical examiner will then proceed to determine whether the drowning was a result of the individual's own failure to stay afloat or the byproduct of some underlying ailment. For this reason, there are educated assumptions which may safely be arrived at when the victim in question is young and healthy, whereas it's not impossible in older people that they may have died in the water as a result of a heart attack or emphysema, or some other serious medical problem.

That makes prompt identification of the body vital to a postmortem medical exam, but, of course, a corpse will always be more deeply probed in those cases where the victim's identity is still not known or the fatality somehow looks and sounds suspicious.

Lying on the examiner's slab and before taking a scalpel to flesh, there are visual clues that can provide a few preliminary answers about the death. For instance, drowning produces a thin foam in and around the victim's mouth which usually lingers there for several days before washing away. The presence or absence of this transient substance, on the other hand, is not conclusive because drug overdoses, electrocutions and strangulations also have the same foaming effect, and because up to 20% of drownings are actually "dry drownings" where the victim took no water into their airways but died instantly, or else suffocated very quickly from a sudden throat-closing reflex.

To see if this telltale foam did once exist, though, placing a hand firmly on the victim's chest and gently compressing it should bring the substance back up once more, perhaps even with pebbles and sand in it. Alternately, when a corpse has begun to decay a darkish, foul-smelling fluid might fill the mouth instead, but this is standard to all types of deaths where putrefaction has set in and is therefore of little diagnostic value. It is the existence of a pair of oversaturated lungs, ideally with debris in them, that will most strongly point to death by drowning. But, again, this by itself is not proof positive either, since a dead body can slowly draw water into its air passages even if only placed in the water after having died elsewhere.

Also, the victim's hands can, and often do, reveal important evidence to a medical examiner. A drowning person grasps at everything within arm's reach to prevent themselves from going under, so they may still be clutching a variety of foreign objects in them. These can be anything they managed to grab hold of before losing consciousness, such as nearby plants, twigs and other artifacts. In fact, this phenomenon is so common, that in some cases it can be considered suspicious if the hands are empty. For example, if the victim's body was entangled in a densely weeded aquatic environment it is reasonable to expect to find them clutching fistfuls of such weeds. Similarly, victims holding things that aren't natural to the settings they drowned in will also be indicative of foul play. And, finally, in very rocky locations, a victim's hands might even be slightly mangled with a missing fingernail or two from scraping against stone to stay afloat.

In death as in life, a person's eyes can tell a story, too. If the victim still has eyeballs in their sockets and these are wide open and glistening, as is usual for bodies found face down in the water, then there is a high probability that they drowned, although this alone won't yet prove whether it was on purpose or by accident. If, instead, a horizontal demarcation "line" is perceptible on each of the eyes (showing distinct cloudy and un-cloudy zones created by postmortem exposure to the air) then they expired, or were killed, someplace on dry land.

Opening the corpse comes next. If the victim truly died in the water then, regardless if it was a dry or wet drowning event, there will always be a considerable volume of watery fluid in the stomach with yet more debris in this mixture, because a person cannot help but to drink water in the final act of drowning. A thorough analysis of the stomach contents is required then and these fluids must be found consistent with a sample of the water the victim allegedly succumbed in. If they are not, this will be determined to be just as suspicious as not finding any such fluid present.

The rapid ingestion and aspiration of large quantities of freshwater and its swift circulation throughout the body will, as well as diluting the victim's blood by as much as 50%, dilute whatever fluids they might have consumed antemortem (prior to the agonal event). Thus, a postmortem toxicology test to determine if any of those might have been intoxicants, and alcohol thereby a culprit in the death, will obviously be thwarted—a blood/alcohol reading from a drowning victim can be drastically lower than what it would have been if measured when the person presumed to be drunk was still alive.

Additionally, taking an accurate BAC from a drown victim is further rendered futile in cases where decomposition has already begun, since alcohol is naturally manufactured in the body through the process of decaying. Consequently, a BAC level in these type of deaths, which on the average requires another month for a lab to process, is not very informative to an experienced and astute medical examiner, especially one who isn't totally convinced that drinking was what caused the individual's drowning.

Signs of trauma to the body, if any, can be equally as perplexing at a glance. While bloody wounds the victim may have received when still living will leach from prolonged soaking and no longer be as noticeable to the naked eye, postmortem injuries a corpse derived from impacts as it traveled along may be much more prominent and deceptively appear as intentional. That's because those latter injuries tend to occur on the more vulnerable parts of the deceased, like the face where a lot of excess blood has collected, and a puncture or tear to these sensitive areas can cause them to ooze profusely.

So too, the whole head of a rotting corpse might totally blacken from all the blood that's shifted to it and congealed, and to the unfamiliar observer this shocking appearance can be mistaken for evidence of having been burnt.

Because all of the foregoing demonstrate that a drowning is never medically clear cut and, often enough, can be simulated to disguise a murder, and because a drowned person may even falsely resemble a murder victim on some occasions, it does demand 100% certainty to officially rule it as the cause of death *and* an accident. This means any lingering doubts a medical examiner still has should and must be disposed of in a more comprehensive autopsy.

There are any number of additional tests which, when performed, can begin to reduce overarching concerns, but a Diatom Test has proved the most decisive in an inquest where the truth of a drowning death still remains shrouded in some mystery.

A diatom, that bountiful microscopic organism found in every single environment on Earth, creates a hard, crusty exterior casing which is virtually indestructible even to decay. Identifying the specific diatoms native to the waters the victim allegedly drowned in and then finding the presence of those diatom breeds in the tissue samples of the victim's organs and in their blood makes it all the more certain that this is the place where the person ultimately died. It also proves the individual did in fact drown and was not placed in that locale after death, since, even if a pre-dead body did take water into the stomach and lungs, there is no way for the dead to circulate water (and that water's microorganisms) throughout all the rest of their systems. Only a living person—or rather a person who is dying—could achieve this, as they're drowning.

After that comparative analysis and matchup is made, if drowning is judged to be the actual cause of death, but the manner itself still cannot confidently be listed as accidental, the death certificate issued will reflect this finding, citing the manner as unknown or undetermined, and the case will then be turned over to the police once again, pending further investigation.

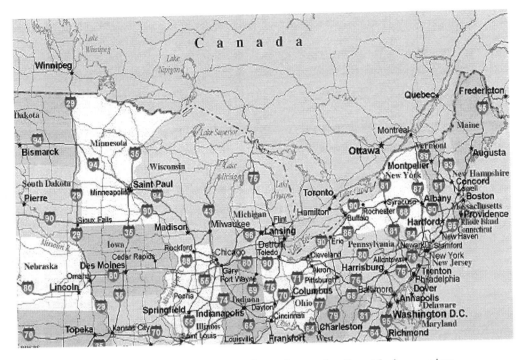

Major US interstate highways in and near the Great Lakes region

Chapter 3: Corridor of Death

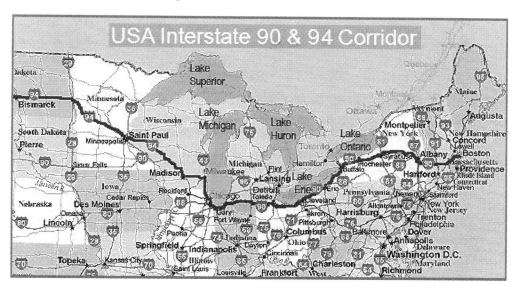

Home to five of the world's largest lakes and many of its mightiest rivers, the territory that stretches from Massachusetts to the Dakotas and which is traversed via the Interstate 90 and 94 thoroughfares, has got to be the most beautiful land on the planet. With its rolling hills and fertile flats and valleys, with its hardwood forests and expansive nature preserves, the freshwater brooks, the mountain streams, the crystal clear lakes and spring-fed ponds, the sunshine…if a place called Valhalla really exists, surely this is it.

Interstates like 90 and 94 in the American north are fairly recent fixtures on the landscape, making it much easier, and certainly a lot faster, to travel from state to state. Decades in the planning, when they first began to be implemented in the late 1950s, road construction crews had to blast through mountains made of solid stone in some places to create these straightaways for us, defy nature to ensure they'd be the most direct routes possible.

Yet, even so, these amazing feats of engineering were themselves constrained by natural forces, each shaped and limited to some degree by the vast waterways that existed here long before their installation. So, although it may be a fact of modern life that superhighways have become king to us, nevertheless, the rivers are still *their* masters. Rivers like the Mississippi and the Wabash and the Hudson cannot be shoved out of the way for the sake of convenience, and they can't be ignored either.

In fact, everything in this watery region of ours must, in one way or another, bend to the will of a river, make a conscious effort to accommodate its presence somehow, to acknowledge and obey its course and character. Right down to the people.

I came of age beside a decent-sized river. In the warm months, ran and biked next to it almost daily, boated it, fished in it, crammed for important exams on its shady banks, and, in the wintertime, skated along its smooth surface for miles and miles in both directions. This was before things started heating up climate-wise, before forty-degree temperature spikes in winter became commonplace. It was much, much colder way back then, back in the days of my more adventuresome youth, and the ice was several feet thick. Perfectly safe to walk on.

There's a weird sigh a frozen river makes at times to relieve the pressure of all that ice that's building in it, a kind of low, taut *twaaang* that comes from above you and beneath you and all around. That sound serves as a subtle reminder of the frigid but still liquid chambers concealed well beneath its icy veneer. A reminder to always be alert and pay very close attention.

Usually when I skated on the river I did so with a pal or two. But not always. Sometimes my classmates and I—as many as a hundred at a time—would throw a skating party down there. Deposit a half dozen beer balls or so, maybe even a full keg, and then build a huge bonfire so we could hang out all night if we wanted to. In fact, summer and winter, we fearlessly partied at the river's edge or on it, or else in lakes and in quarries and in swimming-pools.

And guess what? Drunk or stoned, or any inventive combination thereof, nobody ever drowned.

As a young person, my scholastic interests were primarily in the arts and literature, but at one point I had seriously considered a career in law enforcement. Being athletic, I guess I was attracted to the physicality of that profession. Attracted by the intrigue, too, so I was thinking of maybe training for a job with the FBI or the CIA. As fate would have it, however, it would be those colleges which specialized in the arts and sciences who would woo me. That being the case, I followed the money, so to speak, and, truthfully, never regretted the decision.

Not coincidentally, the university I ultimately chose to attend, though far, far from home, was also situated near a river. A different one this time. Bigger.

Brainiacs and creative types as opposed to jocks and preppies, my fellow students weren't exactly the classic party-school crowd by any means, but, no matter, we sure partied our hearts out. And it wasn't unusual at all to stumble in past dawn, having clubbed through most of the night and, much too wired for sleeping, having hopped all the after-hour spots we could find, too. We'd do that till the sun came creeping over the metropolis and there was no bar left to crash, or none that would have us.

Water, water everywhere, of course, in every single place we strutted or staggered to, and, again, nobody drowned.

As a matter of fact, whether it's a river or a creek or a lake, you'd be hard pressed to find any university, any village or town, any municipality in this particular "neck of the woods" that didn't straddle or cozy up to a major body of water. It's a powerful part of our collective experience, having all this water around us, and because it can both give life and take it away in a flash, we are taught to enjoy *and* respect it.

Or else reap the devastating consequence.

From police to private eyes, from drunkenness to murder, the modern-day mystery of the drowning men has generated many types of theories over the past fifteen years, but, to this date, it has never been solved. The public's interest in this saga waxes and wanes, peaking at times when clusters become more prominent, fading when, predictably, the disappearances and deaths can't be adequately or satisfactorily explained and the authorities raise up their hands in protest declining to entertain any more speculation. They've had it with all the talk of murders and conspiracies, they complain.

I myself have to admit I'm not too big a fan of conspiracy theories, either. That's because I discovered early on in life that most, if not all of them, usually led to a gaping hole about as wide as the Grand Canyon. Yet there's such a pronounced pattern in these "accidental drownings" that, once I finally took notice and began analyzing them, I just couldn't, with any ease, wrap my mind around the concept of a mere coincidence.

With another new year having begun and well over a dozen new cases emerging already, all having the same physical and personality profile, all missing under the same circumstances, it raised my suspicion that, whether due to alcohol or to repetitive acts of malice, something was definitely going on here.

Moreover, with hundreds of such fatalities having now been documented in newspapers and police blotters, I believe any reasonable mind possessing a healthy curiosity would have to agree, it's awfully odd. And being as familiar as I am with the geography and the lifestyle of this particular region just made it seem all the more peculiar.

In trying to get to the bottom of the rivers' riddle, to find which theory provides the answer to so much tragic loss of life, I thought I'd take those professors' joint appeal to heart, apply an objective and critical view toward each argument and see where it all would naturally flow to. This would be an easier task for someone in my position to achieve because I have no ties to any of the victims, no affiliations with any of the investigating parties and agencies, no relationship to the news organizations that covered any of the events. Nothing at stake, and nothing to prove.

As to the subject of proofs, there are mountains of evidentiary facts in this fifteen-year-long case and I compiled and pored over as many different sources as possible: missing person posts, victim profiles, police statements, eyewitness accounts, medical exams, autopsy reports, toxicology findings, newspaper articles, televised interviews, public databases, online discussion threads, photographs, CDC statistics, expert opinions…anything I could think of that would enlighten or help to qualify a remark that was made. Anything that might support or defeat a conclusion.

Although the ending would still be just as sad, this is a story in desperate need of conclusion. However, without much doubt, it begins in 1997 with the inexplicable disappearance and drowning of Patrick McNeill.

"With regard to Patrick McNeill, we have a young man who is found [with] a blood alcohol level of 0.16. Probably a third of that is postmortem putrefaction...a relatively low level of alcohol. There's no way in the world that this man then is accidentally going to fall into a body of water, [and] I'm saying that the fly larvae have been laid in the groin area. It's an indoor fly—could not have been an outdoor fly—it was an indoor fly. And the larvae were there, did not move ahead into the later stage. So we have a body that was already dead before it was placed in the water...I would call it a homicide, yes." *Dr. Cyril Wecht, renowned Forensic Pathologist*

"Circumferentially around the neck there is a pattern which consists of numerous vertical lines evenly spaced (1/16") around his neck as if to suggest some type of binding." *from the McNeill autopsy report by Dr. Charles Hirsch, then Chief Medical Examiner for the city of New York*

"Yes, regarding that particular case in New York, that certainly does sound like it was a homicide." *Candice Delong, career FBI Profiler, speaking of Patrick McNeill's drowning*

"Patrick's death was not an accidental drowning. He was stalked, abducted, held for an extended period of time, murdered, and disposed." *Kevin Gannon, NYPD homicide detective investigating the McNeill case since 1997*

Chapter 4: More Than a Little - Less Than a Lot

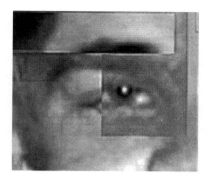

NEW YORK CITY, NEW YORK. – April 17, 1997: "The Fordham University student whose body was found floating near a Brooklyn pier last week died from drowning, New York City's chief Medical Examiner ruled yesterday…he said that the level of alcohol in the body of the student, Patrick McNeill Jr., was 'more than a little and less than a lot'…What remains unclear then is how Mr. McNeill, an athletic 21-year-old, wound up in the river and drowned. The manner of death was listed as undetermined in the autopsy report."

- - -

There are conflicting accounts regarding the last time Patrick McNeill was ever seen alive. Some people said he was only a little bit drunk, and some said he was a lot. Some said he accidentally fell into the East River and drowned himself, and some said he was murdered.

What is agreed upon and substantiated by numerous witnesses and video surveillance is that the 21-year-old was last observed on the evening of February 16th 1997 at an uptown Manhattan bar called the Dapper Dog where he'd been drinking with some of his peers.

The Dapper Dog at that time was a small, narrow college dive that local university students would frequent on the weekends when school was in session. Popular for its frat-like atmosphere, loud music and free-flowing booze, this small pub also attracted its younger patrons with a "guest bartender" night, routinely appointing a popular student to bartend for the evening in hopes he might persuade his circle of friends to stop by for a drink and loosen their wallets.

By 1997 when McNeill and his classmates made the Dapper Dog their official watering hole, its owners had already racked up a considerable number of citations for their laissez faire serving policies. Among the most notable violations, selling alcohol to minors and continuing to serve customers who were visibly and seriously intoxicated. Noise violations were also included in the list of complaints against them, these filed by various neighborhood residents.

One of his college suitemates was the" master of ceremonies" on that February night Patrick McNeill visited The Dapper Dog for the last time in his life. Colleagues of McNeill say he was aware this particular young man didn't care for him very much, but he felt he would be lending some support by showing up anyway. McNeill was a well-liked student otherwise and famous for going out of his way to help people, at the time, involved in at least a half dozen altruistic groups and related activities. A popular social organizer as well, he was also in charge of booking the entertainment acts for Fordham University, so showing up at a place where he may not have been wanted, is probably best viewed within this context.

There were seven roommates in all sharing the Fordham campus suite that McNeill lived in, and more than one of them had openly professed to disliking the 21-year-old intensely, criticizing him to his face and behind his back for being a "womanizer" and complaining that he was always preening himself, that he cared to much for his personal appearance and was obsessed with his academic status.

Standing about six feet tall and weighing in at a well-toned 195 pounds, McNeill was in fact a good-looking, clean cut, athletic guy, and even those who counted themselves among his longstanding friends admitted, "Pat's a real ladies man," adding, "we'd tease him about his clothes, his cologne, how he had to be perfect." As for McNeill's pride in his collegiate accomplishments, one of his professors at Fordham confirmed the third-year undergrad was firmly "on the path for the accounting honor society. It's a step in the direction of his dream," she disclosed, "working for the FBI."

Lofty and reasonable aspirations for a young person to have, especially for an ambitious one who seemed so totally capable of achieving them. If he had not, somehow, been otherwise prevented.

In the early morning hours of the day McNeill went missing, after having just bid everyone goodnight at the Dapper Dog and announcing he was headed for the nearby subway station to return to the Bronx campus, Patrick McNeill was observed lingering out front of the bar for awhile. Allegedly he was waiting there for a female friend who was still inside using the ladies' room but, when she failed to materialize in a timely fashion, he then proceeded down the sidewalk alone, slowly navigating two city blocks until eventually he turned the corner at 90th Street…and disappeared into thin air.

Before that, McNeill's conduct as he had made his way south on Second Avenue from the 92nd Street pub was apparently so worrying that a number of passersby took notice of it, keenly watching as he staggered and sometimes fell down before getting up and stumbling onward again. These eyewitnesses also described a vehicle which appeared to have been shadowing McNeill's movements from the minute he left the Dapper Dog. Suspicious of its driver's intent, one of them, having first seen it double-parked at the bar where McNeill was originally standing, even had the wherewithal to obtain a partial license plate number. Other onlookers also reported their belief that the occupants were tailing the young man, saying the vehicle would come to a complete stop and then resume again each time McNeill would falter. When, in this highly disoriented condition, he finally turned left onto 90th Street, everyone who could see the vehicle at that juncture stated it also took a left.

And neither was ever seen again.

Though the New York Police Department and legions of citizen volunteers searched for Patrick McNeill in the days and weeks following his mysterious disappearance, handing out and hanging up more than 10,000 posters from New York City to Yonkers and in the process making it one of the most famous missing persons cases in the city's history, the young man's fate was not to be learned for months. In the interim, tensions would steadily rise between McNeill's loved ones and the NYPD during the fruitless search, and it wasn't long before the men in blue, who claimed they were being pressured by McNeill Senior's strong republican ties in neighboring Westchester county, began leaking their own opinions about the case, about the victim's character, and his possible whereabouts. Most of these quite negative.

"Patrick made some mistakes," one detective cryptically alluded. "And it appears he needed some time and space to sort things out."

"The kid screwed up," a second NYPD cop emphatically stated. "He's probably hiding out in Queens."

"This kid is 21, he's a partier and he doesn't want to be in college," yet another city detective informed reporters, confiding in them with palpable disdain that he also "knew" Patrick McNeill had impregnated a couple of young women. "He's running around and involved in all this stuff so he doesn't have to be in school," the officer knowledgeably asserted.

One detective from NYPD's missing persons bureau even pointed to the fact that McNeill's ear and tongue were pierced and that the young man had a Celtic cross tattooed on his forearm as proof he was deliberately trying not to be found. "The public wonders why the cops are cynical," the detective wearily opined. "It's because of cases like this."

The Dapper Dog, finding itself in the crossfire and the subject of extreme public and legal scrutiny over their role in serving McNeill on that night, as well as to their dubious record in general, also joined in maligning the victim. "He's shooting heroin on the Westside," they derisively chimed. "But because he's 21 now the cops can't bring him in."

McNeill's discouraged family and friends, placed on the defensive in this way, vehemently disputed these unflattering assessments.

"It's so out of character for my son," McNeill's father insisted. "I know it was foul play."

"If he had problems he'd confide in us. And nothing was bothering him that I know of," a friend who had known McNeill since childhood confidently assured the press.

Even one of his Fordham roommates stated for the record, "I've never seen Pat in a bad mood. He's the last guy who'd run away from a problem."

Things dragged on in this unseemly and unproductive manner well into March of 1997, where the futile search-and-rescue efforts were further exasperated by a series of false sighting in other boroughs of New York. For instance, a real estate agent from Queens reported that someone closely matching the missing man's description stumbled into his office one day looking "disheveled and upset." But this tip, and others like it, though investigated, only amounted to a wild goose chase for the already annoyed police officers of the Bronx precinct, who moaned that their time was being wasted on useless reports that led them nowhere in search of somebody clearly in hiding.

Finally, on April 7th 1997, Patrick McNeill's badly decomposed body, clad only in his blue-jeans and socks, was spotted face up in the East River near a Brooklyn pier, some twelve miles away from his last known location.

Because of the suddenly questionable circumstances surrounding McNeill's death and the condition of his corpse, the case was then tentatively upgraded as a potential abduction and murder pending further investigation by the police. As such, it was transferred from the missing persons department and reassigned to the NYPD's much-decorated homicide detective, Kevin Gannon.

Examining the remains and recovery photos, Detective Gannon had suspected from the body's lack of skin "slippage" that McNeill hadn't been in the water for the entire two months he'd been missing. Maybe, in fact, he'd only been floating around in the river a few days before being discovered. Lividity wasn't adding up, either. The telltale discolorations exhibiting on the front of the corpse clearly showing McNeil had to have died lying face down for all his blood to settle in those parts, whereas his body had been discovered and recovered lying face up.

Knowing from experience, too, that people who accidentally drown aren't usually found floating on their backs, *or with rope burns around their necks and other markings,* the detective was very eager to formally name the yet unidentified owners and occupants of the vehicle seen following the victim as "persons of interest" in the case.

They were not just ogling spectators, Gannon felt certain, and Patrick McNeill had not simply lost his footing and fallen over the dock in some alcoholic stupor. Patrick McNeill hadn't flung off half his clothes in the brutal month of February to take a night swim either, nor restrained himself somewhere with ropes or wires, torched his upper torso and head, dumped his rotting body miles upstream when nobody was around.

The McNeill's had been unlucky to lose their son, but in Kevin Gannon they had at least found a friend in law enforcement, someone just as determined as they were to find justice.

Completely in line with the family's way of thinking, the homicide detective also regarded the intoxicated angle with a great deal of skepticism. If a man McNeill's size, a former high-school football captain, had appeared that wasted on only two or three cocktails, Gannon believed he must've been drugged to make it look that way, slipped a mickey, as they call it in the business. Probably a date-rape narcotic like Rohypnol or GBH, he speculated, colorless substances at that time and virtually tasteless so they couldn't easily be detected when added to a drink. The effects of either Rohypnol or GBH—impaired speech and muscle coordination, blackouts, amnesia—could be quadrupled, even lethal, if mixed with enough alcohol, and both drugs were known to be fast-acting and almost untraceable, even in an autopsy.

So, naturally, Detective Gannon pressed for a "lawman search" to be conducted in order to determine the rest of the numbers on the suspicious vehicle's license plate—

standard operating procedure for a suspected murder. To his surprise, however, the department declined his request, insisting the price tag of $1200, the cost at the time for such a search, was much too costly an undertaking, and especially not warranted where a body exhibiting no major signs of physical trauma greatly diminished the chances of there having been foul play.

It was to be the first of a string of similar investigative setbacks the homicide detective would encounter in trying to solve the McNeill mystery, and when, on April 16th 1997, New York City's chief medical examiner ruled the death an accidental drowning with the manner of death still unknown, Kevin Gannon realized he had a diabolical case on his hands he would never let go of.

Little did he know, within just a few years time, he'd have many more just like it.

"The fact that a MPD officer took Chris' girlfriend home that night (Halloween 2002), and in fact, she was wearing his uniform shirt and hat as a costume…The girlfriend, the cop, the bouncer, getting [Chris] kicked out of the bar, the cop takes her home...do the math."

"I could tell you about how much interference has come our way from members of MPD…I suspect some serious questions might be brought forward to the Mayor of Minneapolis."

Private Detective Chuck Loesch, commenting on his experience investigating the Chris Jenkins 2002 drowning/murder case in Minneapolis

Chapter 5: Cowboys and Indians

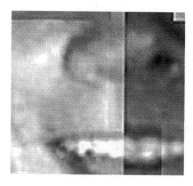

MINNEAPOLIS,MINNESOTA - FEBRUARY 28, 2003: "Authorities pulled the body of missing University student Chris Jenkins from the Mississippi River on Thursday, the family's private investigator reported. A spokesperson for the Hennepin County Medical Examiner's office said two pedestrians saw the body under the Third Avenue Bridge and called police shortly before 4 p.m. Police recovered the badly decomposed corpse approximately two hours later.

Jenkins, a Carlson School of Management student and lacrosse team captain, disappeared from the Lone Tree Bar & Grill at Fifth and Hennepin avenues in downtown Minneapolis on Halloween night. His body was found on the Mississippi River's south bank less than a mile from the bar.

Jan Jenkins, Chris Jenkins' mother, thanked the University community for all its help in searching for her son, but called the police investigation "a serious slap in the face" after they told her Jenkins probably jumped into the Mississippi because he was depressed.

Minneapolis police would not comment Thursday. Sources said the department will make a public statement on Friday."

- - -

In late October of 2002, according to various newspaper and eyewitness accounts, the 21 year-old athletic and popular honor student Chris Jenkins spent Halloween night in full Indian regalia celebrating at the Lone Tree Bar in downtown Minneapolis with his new girlfriend. It appears they may have had some kind of a minor falling out there which seems to have gotten him ejected from the premises shortly thereafter, two closely related events which are alleged to have occurred around midnight.

It happens sometimes that couples don't see eye to eye and they quarrel in public places, especially if it's late, they're tired, and they've both been drinking. But that's no reason to toss a young man into the cold without his keys, wallet, and cell phone.

That's no reason to kill him.

One of the bouncers in charge of keeping things on the up and up at the Lone Tree grill and the adjacent bar on Halloween night was an off-duty Minneapolis cop. It is said that Jenkins' love interest, also an employee of the establishment, was wearing key elements of that officer's official uniform as her own costume, elaborately described in a police report dated November 10, 2002 as consisting of "fishnet shorts, a blue police uniform shirt with patches and badge, and a police hat". Coincidentally, it was to be this same plainclothesman that would end up driving the girl home once the festivities at the Lone Tree had ended and the bar shut down for the evening. As to Chris Jenkins, himself, he would never be seen alive again.

The record of his brief existence before these ominous events played out painted a picture of a responsible youth with a lifelong dedication to his scholastic studies and an equal devotion to his friends and family who he kept in touch with daily. On the fast track to getting his business degree, the University of Minnesota confirmed that Jenkins had a bright future awaiting him, having earned high honors in his classes at their Carlson School of Management and that he was scheduled to graduate within only four years of his beginning attendance there, as opposed to the standard five and a half. Even his girlfriend who'd only known him for two months testified to the same at the Minneapolis police station where she was questioned on November 6th 2002, stating that Jenkins "was driven when it came to his schoolwork and his devotion to the UofM lacrosse team where he was co-captain."

Everyone who reported him missing directed the Minneapolis Police Department to the above facts, further assuring the authorities it was totally out of the ordinary for Chris Jenkins to be away for even 24 hours without making contact with them and expressing their fears for his safety and wellbeing because of the unusual absence.

Yet the MPD declined to commence an immediate search for him, asserting to the Jenkins family that not enough time had lapsed to consider it a missing persons case. Additionally, the MPD told the young man's parents right off the bat that there didn't appear to be any indications whatsoever of foul play in the matter. Days later, when the police finally did launch their investigation into the whereabouts of Chris Jenkins, they seemed to go about it in such a deliberately offhand manner that it threatened to allow the trail to grow cold as they hemmed and hawed with the Jenkins family about certain aspects of the victim's character and basically dawdled.

So the Jenkins did the only other thing they could think of to find their son ASAP: They set up headquarters in the city's downtown section where Chris was last seen, assembled a posse of approximately 100 volunteers to help them search it, and hired a private investigator.

When private eye Chuck Loesch first took on the case, the MPD officers were already dismissing Chris Jenkin' disappearance as a another likely drowning, claiming he must have jumped from, or fell off of, the Hennepin Avenue Bridge into the fast flowing Mississippi River where he quickly drowned. However, video-feed collected from security cameras which had been installed at and around the Hennepin proved this story to be a flippant fabrication at best—Jenkins wasn't seen in any of them.

As a matter of fact, the bloodhounds Loesch obtained for tracking Chris Jenkins' scent didn't pick up anything near the suspect overpass at all, nor below it on the banks of the river. Instead, each separately tracked a trail to a nearby parking garage, and, from there, were led toward the Interstate 94 highway ramp not too far away from it. A few red feathers and some string from Chris' Indian costume spied in parking stalls number 89 and 90 of the underground facility grimly foreshadowed the young man's doom, even as, all the while, the police kept steadfastly insisting he must have drunkenly toppled into the icy waters, either on purpose or by accident, and there were "no signs of foul play."

In all fairness at this point in time, and in order to avoid a glaring conflict of interest or the outright appearance of impeding their own investigation with the object of protecting a colleague from being implicated in it, the Minneapolis police should really have handed off the matter to either another police department. Or, even better, to a higher agency. But they did neither, choosing instead to allow the Jenkins missing persons case to essentially stagnate under their watch, while at the same time stonewalling his family's private detective.

Finally, amidst this endless wrangling, and a full four months after Jenkins had disappeared, his body was spotted floating face up in the Mississippi river under the Third Avenue Bridge, still wearing his Native American costume and the loose fitting shoes that came with it, his shirt tucked neatly into his trousers, his arms folded peacefully across his chest.

But the strands of his own hair clenched tightly in one fist and other subtle evidence of physical trauma revealed Chris Jenkins' finals hours of life to be nowhere near as serene as might be inferred from his frozen pose of death. And, with a postmortem blood/alcohol finding of only 0.07 in his deep tissue and a maximum of 0.12 in his heart, there was very little doubt that, while it might've been true he'd had too much to drink on the night he vanished, he sure wasn't drunk the day he died.

And once more, in a perplexing pattern that was emerging in these cases, there was a drowning with the unresolved issue of exactly how long a period of time—or how short—the corpse had actually been in the water.

Being discovered snagged in debris under the Third Avenue Bridge downtown was also a bit problematic for the MPD since, according to a police report dated November 11th 2002, this specific area had been thoroughly scoured by them before. To wit: "Investigators searched the Father Hennepin Bluffs Park that encloses the bridge on the east bank of the Mississippi. Investigators also searched in the rear of the Main Street post office and underneath the Third Avenue Bridge."

Aggressively sidestepping these curious details, the Minneapolis police quickly ruled the matter an accidental drowning anyway and closed the Jenkins case without further ado, thereafter adamantly refusing to bend on their determination no matter how much new evidence detective Loesch would later come up with. The officials of the city of Minneapolis, just as with other municipalities recently plagued by off-season water fatalities, would then go on to devote more of their time to debunking rumors of murder than to investigating them, and with attempts at minimizing a potential public relations nightmare which was ever so slowly unfolding.

Tall fences. Citizen patrols. More cops on the beat. More cameras. "The waterfront is safe now. There is no serial murderer."

But, Chad, Nathan, Glen, Jeremy, Matthew, Jared, Adam, Dan, Todd, Josh, Jacob, Matt, Lucas, Nicholas, Scott, David...the Jenkins couldn't get the police to reexamine their son's death, and the police couldn't stop more sons from dying.

"When you hear hooves behind you, when you turn around you should expect to see horses, not zebras...the 'horse' diagnosis is 'alcohol' while the 'zebra' diagnosis is 'serial killer' [or] a cop and/or a cab driver..." *University of Wisconsin at La Crosse officials, calling for public calm after yet another disappearance and drowning in 2004*

"It was a classic textbook drowning." *La Crosse County Medical Examiner, publicly commenting in 2004 on the drown victim's autopsy*

Chapter 6: Horses of a Different Color

"Why we are 99.9% sure it is NOT a serial killer – a data based explanation"

"Dear Students, We have both worked here at UW-L for over 10 years. Every time a student has died, we have grieved for the student, his/her family, and friends. We have lost students to fires, auto accidents, suicides, and illness. This semester we lost a student to a drowning. And, again, we grieved, although we did not know him.

"However, within hours of his disappearance, we started to hear theories about the 'serial killer' who prays [sic] on young men in Midwestern college towns with rivers. In response to these theories, we must now be the professors that we are trained to be, as well as the members of the grieving community that we are. Throughout your college careers, you will be asked to engage in critical thinking. Nowhere is critical thinking more important than when you apply your education and training to your own lives and experiences. We implore you to use your critical thinking skills when you look at this situation.

"When medical personnel are trained in the diagnosis of problems, they are often told this story. 'When you hear hooves behind you, when you turn around you should expect to see horses, not zebras.' In other words, the most common event should be the diagnosis you first expect. In the case of Jared Dion and other students who have drowned in the past several years, the 'horse' diagnosis is 'alcohol' while the 'zebra' diagnosis is 'serial killer.' Other zebra diagnoses include the theories that a cop and/or a cab driver are involved in the drownings.

"Let's take a look at some of the data that allow us to feel more secure about the idea that it was a plain old tragic accident that took the life of this student and the others who drowned.

"First, researchers have long been able to identify the development of urban myths (Knight, 2002). Two websites that present lists and analyses of urban legends are Snopes and Urbanlegends. The Snopes website writes that 'A tale is considered to be an urban legend if it circulates widely, is told and re-told with differing details (or exists in multiple versions), and is said to be true.' Scholars believe that individuals are prone to accept stories that do not directly contradict their personal experiences because they have an underlying need to increase their understanding of the world. In addition, conspiracy theories are kin to urban myths. Researchers know that the more 'unexpected' and larger the event is, the more likely the conspiracy theory

(Knight, 2002). Consequently, we don't think that a junkie in New York who overdosed is still alive, but perhaps Elvis Presley might be. We don't think that most folks who die in car accidents were victims of a plot to kill them, but Princess Di was.

"Second, the data have to inform our decisions and how we view this event. If you were to find a squashed mouse in an elephant's cage, how often would you jump to the explanation that a serial killer was involved? The elephant in this case is alcohol. Every single case has involved blood alcohol levels at or above the .20 level. Can many of you name times when you were "totally trashed" and nothing bad occurred? Of course. Nevertheless, that does not negate the fact that we know that alcohol slows the physical and mental responses and mitigates our ability to read and respond to cues.

"The leading cause of death for young men aged 15-24 is unintentional accidents. Men are more likely than women are to die because of an accident. Homicide and suicide are the next two most common causes of death for men aged 15-24. Alcohol has been found to be a factor in many of these events (Hingson, et al., 2002).

"The National Safety Council reports that in 1999, 647 15-24 year-olds died due to drowning, 592 were male. Indeed, males in this age range have a drowning rate that is ten times higher than that of females (3.1 vs. .3 per 100,000, respectively). In comparison, homicide researchers estimate that less than one percent of all homicides are committed by serial killers (Fox & Levin, 1999, p. 167).

"Let's take a look using data. We have 8,148 undergraduates here at UW-L, 3,559 are male. Approximately 40% of males in college binge drink (or drink to get drunk) regularly (Hingson, et al., 2002). Data from 567 UW-L students suggests that 32% of UW-L males reported having 6 or more drinks the last time they partied. Therefore, on any given Friday night in downtown La Crosse there may be up to 1,140 very drunk 18-24 year old male UW-L students downtown. Even if the number of male UW-L students downtown was one-tenth of this estimate, there would be 114 drunken UW-L males downtown. Many may wander about after the bars close, some will wander toward the river. Every now and then, someone will fall in and drown.

"What about the 'coincidences'? Let's take a close look at these. They are what we call in the social sciences 'illusory correlations' – things that may appear related but are not or are explained by other events. Several websites now advance the theory that there is a serial killer loose in the upper Midwest praying on young college men [indicating] the following 'coincidences' among the victims:

- *Mostly White males between the ages of 17-27*
- *Lived in Minnesota, Wisconsin, Michigan, Indiana or Chicago the area surrounding Lake Michigan*
- *Mostly students or recent graduates*
- *Most were high-achieving*
- *Most were in good physical condition or athletes*
- *Last seen out drinking with friends or at a party*
- *Were under the influence of alcohol*
- *Became separated from the friends with whom they started the evening*
- *All disappeared between the hours of 10 PM and 4 AM*
- *Were reported missing by friends or family*
- *The closed cases were all determined to be accidental drowning or possible suicides*
- *Many of those found drowned were found in the Mississippi River, Red Cedar River or Lake Michigan*
- *Victim's body, if found, had no signs of strangulation - gunshot - stab or other obvious sign of murder*
- *All disappeared between the months of September and April.*

"Where is the coincidence with these numbers? These are college towns with rivers. In college towns, there are many college-aged males. The upper Midwest is overwhelmingly European American. College men who drink tend to do so in bars. College men who drink tend to do so from 10 pm -4 am and between the months of September and April. Easily 30% of college males might match these characteristics. If you go back to our conservative estimate of 114 drunk male college students downtown, that would be 34 men every Friday night who fit the 'coincidence' profile.

"We've both heard a lot of questions the past few days.

"Q: 'Why don't more students drown in Madison?' A: Madison has a lake not a river. It gradually becomes deeper and is not moving swiftly.

"Q: 'Why would he go to the river?' A: Is it really so hard to imagine? He feels drunk. He thinks walking in the fresh air will 'clear his head.' He walks in the direction of the river. He feels nauseous and leans over the river to vomit, or he decides to splash his face with water. He slips. The river is 18 feet deep and moving rapidly.

"Q: 'Why aren't there female victims?' A: Women are much more likely to be socialized to the dangers of being alone – especially while drinking. They have learned, and use, elaborate systems for checking on one another when going downtown or into other situations where they might be vulnerable to victimization.

"Does any of this make Jared's death any less tragic? No. However, we should not jump to the extremely unlikely explanation that a serial killer is responsible rather than the extremely likely explanation that his death is an unfortunate mix of a high level of intoxication and a cold, swift river. Perhaps even more of a concern is that it is somehow more comforting for us to think that Jared's death was caused by something we cannot control (e.g., a serial killer) rather than a cause we can control (not getting drunk, always keeping an eye on your buddies to ensure their safe return home). It is often harder to accept explanations that hit close to home - explanations that involve actions we ourselves have engaged in that put us at risk.

"We join you in your grief, but we urge you to use your critical thinking skills. For each of the questions you hear or ask, please try to think of the types of information you would need to know to help think through the various theories and hypotheses. We encourage you collectively to take action to prevent events like this from happening in the future. For example, what can you as an individual student do to prevent accidents and deaths that are alcohol related? How could the student body work together with the city of La Crosse to make the river's edge and drinking downtown safer (such as the safety bus)?

"Finally, we encourage you to make use of campus resources to assist you in the grieving process and in your education about alcohol and its consequences."

Signed:

Betsy Morgan, Ph.D., Chair of Psychology with an ongoing interest in cognitive biases.

Kim Vogt, Ph.D, Chair of Sociology and Archaeology with a research specialty in homicide

2004

Chapter 7: Profile of a Murderer

Even in the summer months or in the warmer southern regions, people don't generally swim in rivers. They prefer to boat on them or to fish from the safety of the shore, or maybe, now and then, if up to a challenge, do some whitewater rafting. But, aside from these recreational activities, sensible folk rarely venture into a river's churning waters to so much as dip their toes.

A river is deadly, not only because it's deep and murky, with all kinds of unknown things floating on the surface or submerged just beneath it, but because it's swift moving as well, its powerful and constantly shifting currents posing the risk of death even for the strongest of swimmers.

This is the nature of a river. Summertime or winter, it can kill.

Here in the Great Lakes region of the United States our rivers are nearly impassable in the winter months, frozen so thick in various locations that even commercial boating traffic grinds practically to a halt. Then, as they begin their rapid thawing in the springtime, the rivers dangerously swell over their banks, ravaging the shoreline with ragged chunks of ice; these massive flows sometimes jamming so badly in places that many communities located close by or downstream to them are threatened with flash-flooding.

Flooding *is* our Spring.

Of the many U.S. rivers, the Mississippi with its major tributaries is the largest river system in America, draining all or part of 32 states and nearly dissecting the country in half. It's also the third longest in the world, at more than 3800 miles in length dwarfed only by the Amazon and the Nile.

Nourished in the north by the Missouri, the Illinois and the Ohio rivers, and along the way by the Arkansas, the Red and the Tennessee, the immense Mississippi River itself has its primary source in the uppermost mid-western state of Minnesota, at a place 1500 feet above sea level called Clearwater County. There it begins to flow from Lake Itasca and, meandering south from this point, continues to collect fresh water from an estimated 40% of the United States' landmass. All of which is emptied into the Atlantic Ocean at the Gulf of Mexico.

Minnesota, Wisconsin, Iowa, Illinois, Missouri, Tennessee, Arkansas, Mississippi, Louisiana—whatever state you view it from—it seems immovable, this vast and awesome waterway. Yet even it has changed its course at times, throughout thousands of years, whenever it became clogged and inefficient, seeking a better, more direct route to its conclusion, and once more setting itself right.

"Todd died no more than 48 to 72 hours before his body was recovered. This is not consistent with the original finding that Todd died the night he disappeared and was in Ovidhall Lake for 21 days." *Former New York State District Attorney Trish DeAngelis, requesting the 2005 Todd Geib drowning case be reopened and investigated as a homicide*

"Someone is out there, walking around, that killed my son. I have no doubt. This is something we are not letting go until we have justice for Todd." *Kathy Geib, mother of drowning victim Todd Geib*

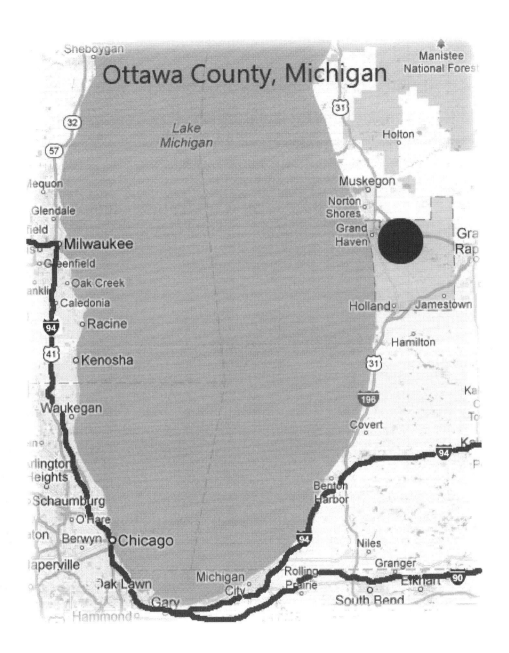

Chapter 8: Gradual and Not Swift Moving

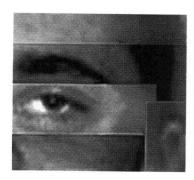

MICHIGAN- MARCH 18, 2010: "An Ottawa County mother tonight says she has proof her son did not accidentally drown in 2005 but was murdered, and wants police to take a new look at his case."

- - -

The Great Lakes cover an enormous swath of real estate in North America, their deep, cold waters keeping things cool or frigid in the northland for nearly ten months out of the year. Things don't really begin to heat up in this watery territory until July and August when, with all the humidity that the region builds, a scorching summertime arrives which is characteristically sticky and muggy. But it is a brief heat, oppressive as it might feel at times, and more than welcome. Then, toward the final weeks of September, with the hours of daylight suddenly decreasing, everything abruptly starts to cool again and a showy but short autumn descends before the deep freeze sets in.

It's still late spring up here in May and June. The days are mild and the nights cool but pleasant. Daytime temperatures are gradually rising as summer slowly advances, though, and, as the mercury starts to climb, the rivers and lakes are steadily getting warmer, too.

But they're still pretty cold in the first weeks of June. A bit too unbearable yet for swimming.

On June 11th of 2005, outdoor enthusiast Todd Geib, 22, was last seen alive leaving a bonfire party in Muskegon County, Michigan, heading on foot for his nearby residence. His final contact with friends was sometime after midnight when he placed an emergency cellphone call in which he reported having difficulty breathing and being "lost in a field."

An unsuccessful search was launched for him when it was determined he was missing, but by June 27th the local police had begun informing news reporters and Geib's family that they had information from unnamed sources that Todd had been hit by a car and buried somewhere.

However, regardless of this quasi-official version of his whereabouts, three weeks after Geib mysteriously disappeared, a couple discovered his body in Ovidhall Lake in Casnovia Township, a rural, wooded section already extensively searched by at least 1500 rescue personnel and community volunteers.

Promptly thereafter, with autopsy and toxicology reports still pending, police ruled the death a drowning due to over-intoxication and closed the investigation as an accident.

But Todd Geib's mother all along believed her son to be the victim of foul play and repeatedly requested the police investigation into his death be reopened and completed. She felt the suspicious circumstances of her son's alleged drowning were completely identical with a number of other regional cases in which young men vanished into thin air and then were found dead in nearby water many weeks or months later, and that, similarly, her son's case was not given the thorough review it deserved from law enforcement.

It was with those beliefs lodged firmly in their hearts that the Geib family ultimately enlisted the aid of seasoned investigator and attorney Trish DeAngelis, asking her to review their son's case and to assist them in their pursuit of justice.

A former New York District Attorney, DeAngelis agreed, upon close scrutiny of the Geib files, that there were many troubling inconsistencies which merited further investigation by the police. She then delivered Todd Geib's autopsy report and related attachments to Dr. Michael Sikirica, a board certified Forensic Pathologist and CEO of Forensic Identification and Profiling Laboratory who, in turn, consulted with his own team of experts as well as others in the medical profession.

Sikirica also went another step further and shared the file at an international convention of Medical Examiners, with the result that more than 200 of those attendees agreed with his final findings: Todd Geib was dead for only two to five days of the entire three weeks he'd been missing.

In a letter then sent to Muskegon County Prosecutor Tony Tague and dated October 7, 2009, former D.A. DeAngelis stated she was absolutely convinced by the body of evidence, "that Todd died no more than 48 to 72 hours before his body was recovered," and that the autopsy and recovery photos, including the postmortem blood/alcohol level of only 0.12 percent, simply could not support the original finding of an accidental drowning, nor that Todd Geib died the night he disappeared.

Prosecutor Tague forwarded that letter to the Michigan State Police for renewed consideration, but, after three months, the police informed the Geib family they had no intention of reopening Todd Geib's case.

The Geib family has since launched a Facebook campaign in hopes of overturning that decision. View their Facebook profile page for more information about the late Todd Geib or to join their efforts to persuade the police to *Reopen Todd Geib's Case* @ http://www.facebook.com/pages/Re-Open-Todd-Geibs-Case/105823769445125

"It's not just a smiley face. He's evil, happy and he drew horns which are synonymous with the devil. He's telling you he knows murder is evil," investigator Kevin Gannon declared. "It's an organized killer which hunts his victims and takes real pride in what he does."

Chapter 9: Drowning Out the Opposition

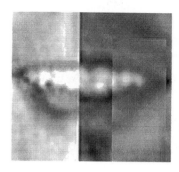

In one way or another the Smiley Face Murders have claimed a great many casualties through the years, and retired NYPD Sergeant Kevin Gannon, the "father" of the Smiley Face Killer theory, must surely consider himself to be one of them.

But the résumé of Kevin Gannon's twenty-year career with the New York Police Department speaks volumes about the man's integrity, no matter how mired in controversy he may have become over time, and it reads just like a page from Who's Who in law enforcement.

Officer Gannon was twice decorated with the Medal of Valor and retired from the NYPD as a Sergeant in the Detective Bureau, with specialties in diversified security, investigative work, police management, major disaster preparedness, and electronic and physical surveillance. During his years of service to the force he was also entrusted with providing travel/security details for such high-profile individuals as Mother Teresa, Prime Minister Barak of Israel, Prince Nawaf of Saudi Arabia, President Putin of Russia, President Fidel Castro, Microsoft executive James Allchin, Vice President Gore, and President Clinton.

In the NYPD homicide division back in 1997 when the first drown victim, Patrick McNeill, had disappeared, Detective Gannon was still working that case in retirement, still operating on the theory that the young man hadn't died by accident and hoping someday soon he'd get the chance to prove it. In so doing, deliver closure to McNeill's grieving parents who also believed their son had been murdered.

As things stood in the McNeill investigation many years later, murder still remained a fuzzy theory that the NYPD wasn't buying into, but it was a theory which would solidify considerably for Gannon once he got word of another case dating from 2003 almost just like it. This latter one, located way out in America's heartland, in the northern state of Minnesota, was going to be the big break Gannon was looking for. He had a good gut feeling about this, and he could always rely on that instinct.

If you've ever had the opportunity to observe an officer of the law operating on a gut feeling, then you probably couldn't help but notice, whether they're wrong or they're right, a cop with a hunch is like a dog with a bone. And, by the mid 2000's, Gannon was especially so motivated because, during the years since McNeill's death, he'd tracked other dubious drownings of college-age men in the area, discovering in dozens of such cases, stretching from New York to Minnesota, an established pattern that deeply troubled him. Aspects that linked them beyond victim profiles and the cause of death.

The writing was literally on the wall, Gannon felt. Scrawled in the form of odious song lyrics, smiley faces, and anonymous initials. By all outward appearances, it very much looked to him like the northland had a vicious and cunning serial killer at large. A group of them acting in concert, he believed, who, in classic serial killing style, were proudly leaving their signature at many of the murder scenes.

Boasting.

Those victim numbers were starting to really add up, too, and Detective Gannon was relieved to learn that he was not the only one anymore to have noticed a sudden geographical predisposition for non-recreational drownings. Many of the affected communities in the northern U.S. district had started voicing their own concerns about a systematic slaughtering of young men. Some doing it in hushed tones from private quarters or hurriedly over the telephone, others shouting it loudly at public meeting halls so they could be heard above a growing din. Thus, by the time Chris Jenkins' body was recovered from the icy Mississippi in the early months of 2003, most everyone in that part of the country had already been referring to such fatalities as the "I-94 Murders".

They didn't yet know just how large an area was afflicted by these events, nor anything about telltale, cryptic graffiti.

They didn't know Team Gannon was on the case.

And what a spooky case it was, Gannon thought he'd uncovered. Placing dead men into frigid waters, often where the individuals were last observed to be socializing, would make these so called accidents near-perfect crimes, he realized. Ostensibly, there would be nothing suspicious about a supposed drunk falling through thin ice and succumbing to hypothermia.

An experienced investigator working in one of the most crime-ridden cities on the planet, he knew as well how quickly water washes away valuable clues such as fingerprints and fibers. It can even, under some circumstances, if the bodies are in it long enough, destroy any delicate signs of physical trauma. That belied the evil brilliance of it all, because, without evidence of blunt force trauma or other internal and external injuries, it would be standard protocol for police of any sized municipality to rule out foul play, and to chalk up incident after incident as the unfortunate byproduct of binge drinking.

The only way to solve a murder is to first suspect it, to search for its clues in and on a body until you find them, because, realistically, no crime is perfect and homicide always leaves a mark. If you know where to look for it.

But medical examiners, like cops, also have protocol to follow, and a major part of theirs is a reliance on the initial reports handed to them by police as to the condition of a body when recovered and the circumstances of how it ended up where it was found. More often than not, this tepid approach isn't out of laziness but a necessity, since the deeper one digs for evidence in a corpse, the more costly the inquest becomes. In short, lawmen and medical examiners, as with most everyone else, have fixed budgets, and murder can be expensive.

Savvy investigators are always conscious of these constraints and know a predetermination by law enforcement officials of "accident" would be all the more likely in cases of apparent drownings, since a murder-by-drowning motif is virtually unheard of in homicide, and because the target group for this type of death was clearly young males known to have been partying into the wee small hours of the morning.

If you are convinced you're hot on the heels of an unorthodox killer, it's frustrating coming up against these biases, but they don't necessarily represent sloppy police work either, since mortality rates and causes are in fact measured in probabilities and statistics, and, statistically speaking, it's not improbable at all for males between the ages of 15 and 24 to meet up with some tragic end by their own foolish devices.

A male in the blush of youth, therefore, particularly one retrieved from a lake or a river after painting the town red with his friends, won't usually get a comprehensive autopsy, despite that he wasn't swimming or boating or skating or suicidal, or even originally headed in the direction of the water when last observed.

And, coincidentally, be they absolutely blind drunk at the moment they died or stone cold sober, a related toxicology report will always register a higher than normal blood/alcohol content in the deceased, *because alcohol is manufactured through decomposition.*

Anybody with a background in law enforcement or a connection to the profession would know this stuff. You didn't need to be some high-ranked ex-NYPD homicide detective to be privy to it, just one smart killer who's done his homework on the subject. Smart, and very, very wicked.

Though he firmly believed it was not just one such individual but a national gang of them on a lengthy crime spree, Detective Gannon still wasn't sure yet who the devious criminals could be displaying such an intimate knowledge of police procedures and forensics. Only that they were dangerously demented and had to be stopped at all costs.

So he mortgaged his home that he might continue to give them chase.

Meanwhile, on the opposite end of the killing fields, in the state of Minnesota, a private investigator holding the same convictions as Gannon held was, on behalf of Chris Jenkins' bereaved parents, steadily whittling away at the Minneapolis Police Department's flimsy account of their son's 2002 "accidental drowning" in the Mississippi River and challenging MPD's refusal to further investigate it.

Week by week, month by month, Gannon's counterpart in Minneapolis, Chuck Loesch, was amassing enough evidence to show the MPD's ruling of "no signs of foul play" had either been reached as a result of epic ineptitude or by a deliberate whitewash of similar proportions.

Significant among this detective's findings was the fact that bloodhounds on two separate occasions each traced Chris Jenkins' scent from the Lone Tree bar, where he was last seen alive, to a hidden location *away* from the bridge in question and far from the river's edge.

People can hide or distort the facts, but dogs, never, Loesch emphasized. They have no reason to:

"The dog took us into the parking area," he unequivocally stated. "The dog took us down to these stalls here. Both dogs did. One was within six days of Chris missing, the second was about three to four weeks later." He told the MPD the bloodhounds further indicated that Jenkins got into a vehicle which then headed west onto Interstate 94.

With the same degree of tenacity as Kevin Gannon displayed in pursuing the McNeill case, Chuck Loesch persevered for years in the Jenkins investigation. Finally, in 2006, based on his outstanding footwork, he met with success: The Chris Jenkins' case was officially reopened by the Minneapolis Police Department, upgraded to a homicide, and a long overdue public apology for the delay, straight from the mouth of Chief of Police himself, was issued to the victim's family.

Yet, unbelievable as it may seem after all that, the MPD still took no significant action to solve the crime, and, to this day, no charges have ever been filed against anyone. Not a single person has ever been detained or arrested on suspicion of involvement. This murder case, thwarted from day one, has since grown all but cold with official neglect.

The Jenkins family themselves, triumphant at last but emotionally exhausted and totally disgusted with the MPD's continued apathy, then handed the entire matter over to Gannon and his team of experts who, by this date, were already fully familiar with the Jenkins affair, having established similarities with a number of other such deaths throughout the northern corridor.

Mrs. Jenkins has since written and released a book titled *Footprints In Courage* chronicling the ordeal of her son's disappearance and death and the long drawn out battle to get the police to find his killers. To peruse and purchase it from Amazon's Kindle store visit: http://www.amazon.com/dp/B003VPWW4I

Kevin Gannon, on the other hand, relentlessly continued his pursuit of justice for all the families and victims concerned, staking everything he had on the outcome. Including his own reputation.

"They made my son out to be a criminal and not a victim," Josh Szostak's father said. He claimed the Albany Police Department, who closed the case within only a few hours of retrieving the young man's body from the Hudson River, also accused him of drawing the smiley face graffiti found on the riverbank, in order to keep his son's story alive.

The Albany Police reported that, "Investigator Bell stated he found no text messages in his phone," but Szostak's father said the Bethlehem Police Department, who shared jurisdiction over the case, had actually taken a photo of it. "Somebody had to erase his messages," he insisted. "The photograph of the cellphone showed it had eight new messages."

"Based on the totality of the case and an autopsy report, this was an accidental drowning," said Detective James Miller of the Albany Police Department. "It is a tragic accident. That is all it is."

Chapter 10: Smiling Faces

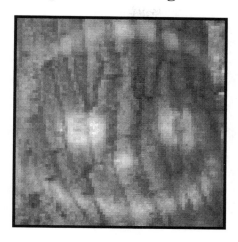

ALBANY, NEW YORK - April 22, 2008: "Police believe a body found in the Hudson River is that of Joshua Szostak. The 21-year-old college student at Plattsburgh disappeared two days before Christmas after spending the evening in downtown Albany with his friends."

- - -

By the year 2007, due to the harsh new reality of the threat of terrorism and a steady rise in violent crime, surveillance cameras had become a fixture of life in the United States. Whereas, only one decade earlier, in the last part of the 20th century, this kind of technology wasn't that commonplace. Major banks might have had such devices installed, automatic-teller machines, toll booths on the interstate, large commercial enterprises.

But today security systems are in use everywhere one goes. In parking lots and supermarkets, restaurants, government buildings, private homes, town squares, the local bar…people are protecting themselves now. Everybody's clandestinely watching what's going on around them, making a visual record of it, protecting their most valuable assets. Similarly, whenever out and abroad themselves, they're being protected in this manner, too. Or watched just as closely.

Joshua Szostak's last hours of life, as he knew it, were captured on hidden cameras. On the night of December 22, 2007, he was shown, first, happily downing a few drinks with his friends over the course of a few hours at a North Pearl Street establishment in downtown Albany, New York called the Bayou Cafe.

There, he was laughing and listening to music and consumed three or four beers in all, as judged from viewing the indoor surveillance feed filmed above the bar.

That's not a large quantity in the scheme of things, as anyone who's ever consumed alcohol at a social gathering would know. Certainly not enough to make a man of Szostak's stature—about six feet tall and 200 pounds—overly intoxicated, to the point of falling down.

Around midnight, Szostak was observed with a male acquaintance making his way through the crowd to go outdoors. A camera fixed from right across the street furnished a grainy account of what took place from there: The two young men chatted for a brief moment in front of the Bayou on the sidewalk (left of center of the screen) and then the other male politely bid adieu to Szostak and headed off, leaving him standing outside alone.

Szostak seems all right, though. Displaying no problems as yet, although why he originally left the bar is still not discernible. Perhaps the place felt stuffy and he just needed a breath of fresh air, or maybe he decided to go home. Perhaps he just wanted to call somebody and it was too loud inside to talk on the phone.

We do see him suddenly rummaging through his clothes, presumably for his cellphone, and possibly removing an object that size from one of his pockets.

In the meantime, cars cruise past him coming from both directions, an assortment of marked vehicles mingled among them including a couple of taxis. Other bar patrons are also milling about, standing around and behind him in pairs or in groups as pedestrians cross the street to and from the bar. Some couples, some trios, some individuals as well.

Frankly, it's not very exciting footage so far, and nothing looks too terribly out of the ordinary either. Not for a Saturday night in the city. Until Szostak suddenly lurches forward and doubles over as if in pain, staggers to his feet once more, and begins struggling inexpertly to pull his coat off.

Here we can see some signs of physical discomfort, but we can't tell what's causing it. He acts confused now, too, stumbling slightly as he begins to gravitate away from the front of the bar, moving in the videotape from the left side of the screen slowly toward the right and hesitating on the sidewalk for a few seconds to once more wrestle with his coat (which for a split second almost looks like he has on backwards). Finally, with the coat adjusted properly, he exits the screen to the right.

Reportedly, his car was parked only about a block or two from the Bayou Café that night, so it is safe to assume that's where Szostak was going next. For him to end up at the Hudson River in the exact spot where his cellphone was found later—on the ground at the Port of Albany—he would have had to change direction to get to the riverbank and then continue walking in his groggy condition south along the river, for at least another two miles.

We know for certain he didn't do that because his image was caught on a second surveillance camera only a couple of minutes later at the intersection of North Pearl and State Street, just where and when he'd have been expected to arrive if everything was normal.

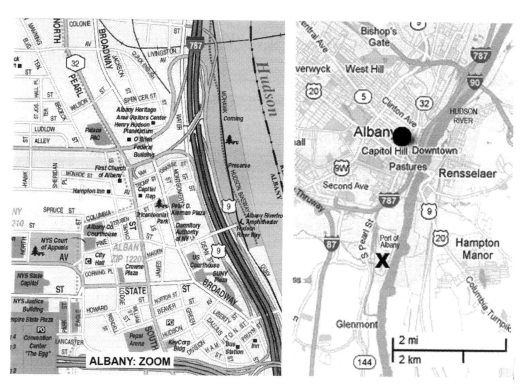

However, shortly after this sighting, something clearly must have gone wrong for Szostak, because where he should have been taped by other cameras along that trek, he wasn't. Nor did the Albany police find any further documentary evidence showing he continued on down Pearl Street beyond the State Street intersection, or that he took an alternate route on foot to some other destination.

As a matter of fact, Joshua Szostak never even made it as far as to his own car in the early morning hours of December 23rd 2007, and, from his last videotaped location, was never seen alive again.

But this story gets even stranger…

Around the same time Szostak was leaving the Bayou Cafe, a few miles outside the city limits, near the Port of Albany on the Hudson River, a surveillance camera at the State Department of Environmental Conservation facility videotaped someone stealing a DEC vehicle from the parking lot.

Thereafter, two more cameras at that same location tracked the thief or thieves driving it to a nearby desolated spot directly on the waterfront, and where, oddly enough, police claim no other cameras were positioned.

There, the driver rammed down a locked gate to enter a restricted zone and, once inside, quietly parked the stolen SUV and abandoned it, apparently leaving no clues as to their motive for the theft or whether they immediately walked away or were rendezvousing with another automobile.

Soon after this event, according to police reports, at approximately 1:40 AM on December 23, 2007, the stolen DEC vehicle was retrieved from this site. It had sustained substantial damage to its undercarriage from the impact of the gates and from barreling over them. Not incidentally, the front of the DEC building, which itself had not been broken into, would be where Szostak's cellphone was recovered. Although, at this specific date, he had not yet been reported missing.

It does seems hard to believe, in light of the above occurrence, that the Albany police weren't already on the lookout for Joshua Szostak *before* his family actually reported him missing, but apparently they were not. Once the Szostak's did contact the APD about their son's disappearance, however, the department was quick to link the two incidences, informally identifying the young man as their primary suspect in the crime and only slightly stepping back from this assertion when a fingerprint sweep of the front portions of the DEC vehicle ruled him out and otherwise proved "inconclusive".

"He's a happy-go-lucky kid," Joshua Szostak's aunt informed the press when interviewed about her nephew's puzzling disappearance. Something bad had to have happened to keep him away so long, she assured reporters. It wasn't like him at all. "He's obligated to his family. He's obligated to his job. He's obligated to his academics and his schoolwork," she said. "It's totally out of character. Totally out of character."

In conducting their own search of the downtown vicinity during the days and weeks that followed, Szostak's parents each publicly expressed frustration and outrage at the way the local police department was handling the case, accusing the APD of being too lackadaisical about the case and of portraying their son more like a criminal than a victim.

Mrs. Szostak even claimed the Albany police had actively sought to discourage her and her husband from gathering community volunteers to help in the early search-and-rescue effort. But a spokesman for the Albany police, upon hearing that, quickly countered the accusation, and adamantly insisted the APD had already employed K-9 and mounted search units as well as helicopters and state-of-the-art sonar as soon as it was feasible for them to do so, and had found nothing more to go on.

This well publicized acrimony would lead to a more and more fractious relationship between the Szostak's and the Albany police as the weeks of searching turned into months and the family's hopes turned into fears.

When, finally, on April 22nd 2008, Joshua Szostak's body was discovered drifting downstream in the Hudson River in another part of the state, it was with disappointment and heavy hearts that his family brought him home once again for autopsies and burial.

The Albany Police Department, clearly relieved and eager to conclude the matter, succinctly closed the case that very same day Szostak's corpse was retrieved from the water, and cited accidental drowning as the cause of death, with no signs whatsoever of foul play.

Postmortem toxicology results delivered many weeks later showed only a 0.126 blood/alcohol level in the deceased and Szostak's father, a skilled arson investigator himself, had in the interim come across other reports which additionally provoked doubts about the true cause of his son's death and the veracity of the APD's claims.

In the newspapers, he'd also been reading about an ex-NYPD homicide detective who was talking about a gang of serial killers drowning college age males in the region and sometimes leaving smiley-faced graffiti on the water's edge. So Mr. Szostak got into his car and followed the river into the next county where his son's body had been recovered, to see for himself if there was a connection.

A new smiley face spray painted on a nearby tree, an inexplicable four month long disappearance, and a questionable drowning under extremely questionable circumstances…Szostak contacted Kevin Gannon without delay, and thereafter vowed never to give up investigating his son's death until he had all the answers.

He is still hunting for the truth, even today, and has established a website for posting updates on the case and for receiving anonymous tips from the public. To learn more about his late son and to view a clip of video surveillance from that night in December of 2007 when Joshua Szostak was last seen leaving the Bayou Café, visit www.JoshuaSzostak.com. All information submitted there is reviewed and considered confidential.

Chapter 11: Prime Time for a Killing Theory

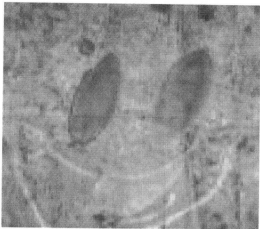

2008 extract courtesy CNN *transcripts.cnn.com*

LARRY KING, *CNN* ANCHOR HOST: Next, they're calling them the Smiley Faced murders now happening. But are they murders at all? It's puzzling. We'll talk about it with police, a victim's family and crime experts, right after this.

[COMMERCIAL BREAK > RETURN TO HOST]

KING: Now this is puzzling. The so-called Smiley Faced murders involve the deaths of dozens of men. But are they really homicides? The debate has torn families and law enforcement apart. Take a look.

[VIDEO + VOICEOVER]

KING: Thirty five suspicious deaths in 33 cities, all men under the age of 30, found dead after a night of drinking with friends. Another link, this symbol, a smiley face painted near some of the bodies. The men were all eventually discovered in lakes or rivers. Coincidence? Or the work of serial killers?

KEVIN GANNON, FORMER NYPD SERGEANT: These young men are being abducted by individuals in the bars, taken out and, at some point, even held for a period of time before they are entered into the water.

KING: Retired Sergeant Kevin Gannon began his investigation in 1997, when the body of 20-year-old Patrick McNeil was found floating off a pier in Brooklyn. He was last seen with friends in a bar in Manhattan. Dozens of suspicious deaths have followed along with the haunting symbols...

[CUT TO HOST > CONTINUE VIDEO VOICEOVER]

KING: Local officials ruled most of the deaths accidents. But Gannon and fellow retired detective Anthony Duarte say they have even more evidence tonight that proves these men didn't drown, that they were murdered.

[END VIDEO]

KING: The aforementioned Kevin Gannon and Anthony Duarte join us. Kevin is the retired New York PD detective. He's been tracking suspicious drownings of scores of young men all over the country. He's in New York. So is Anthony Duarte, the retired New York PD detective. He's working with Gannon on what some are calling the Smiley Face murders. And in Tampa is Dr. Cyril Wecht, forensic pathologist and attorney. He's examined autopsy reports from some of the cases that Gannon and Duarte are investigating.

Kevin, is the reason you think this is murder the smiley face nearby at all the deaths?

GANNON: That's not the only reason. Obviously, we did a lot more work than that. Besides the specificity of the group, that is so narrowly related to age, 19 to 23, highly intelligent, all very athletic young men. But besides that, we had to do all of the evidentiary work that would try to substantiate our claims that these are homicides and not just mere coincidences with a smiley face attached to it.

KING: Anthony, you have suggested these were perfect crimes. What was the typical cause of death listed on the death certificate?

ANTHONY DUARTE, FORMER NYPD POLICE DETECTIVE: Many times it was listed as either accidental or possible suicide. And in many cases, it was also listed as undetermined.

KING: What told you it was murder?

DUARTE: Well, we think in somewhere around twelve cases, we have enough evidence now that we can point it towards murder.

KING: Like?

DUARTE: Like in the Patrick McNeil case that we currently are here for, we have new evidence that we just got from the autopsy report and photos, showing that unfortunately Patrick was burned, and has a ligature on him. And this suggests to us that the medical examiner's office missed this, and this case should have been classified as a homicide.

KING: So Dr. Wecht, what they're saying is a serial killer is loose, kind of a brilliant serial killer, who can beat forensic experts. You have examined some autopsy reports. What do you make of this?

DR. CYRIL WECHT, FORENSIC PATHOLOGIST: Larry, first of all, if I may say from a forensic, epidemiological standpoint, as you pointed out in your introduction, the statistics are so stacked against this number of men, young men, Caucasian males, found in bodies of water in that cluster of states, within that period of time…

From the forensic pathology standpoint, with regard to Patrick McNeil, we have a young man who is found—he has a blood alcohol level of 0.16. Probably a third of that is postmortem putrefaction, a quarter to a third of that. So we have a relatively low level of alcohol. There's no way in the world that this man then accidentally is going to fall into a body of water, because he has a 0.1 or a 0.12 level of alcohol.

Then he has fly larvae, that's the key thing, Larry. It brings in anthropology and entomology with pathology. Fly larvae are found in his groin. These are fly larvae that could not have been laid in that area of the body postmortem.

KING: In English, what are you saying?

WECHT: I'm saying that the fly larvae have been laid in the groin area. It's an indoor fly—could not have been an outdoor fly—it was an indoor fly. And the larvae were there, did not move ahead into the later stage. So we have a body that was already dead before it was placed in the water.

KING: I got you. You're saying he was murdered?

WECHT: I would call it a homicide, yes.

[CUT > COMMERCIAL BREAK > RETURN & CUT TO HOST]

KING: So Kevin, what we're saying here, Kevin, is—you're saying that there's a serial killer out there right now?

GANNON: Well, this isn't just one individual.

KING: How do you know?

63

GANNON: Because of the fact that we have a multiplicity of victims on same dates across the country. The fact that what I was trying to tell people before about the evidentiary—we went to find this evidence; we looked at the location of the body, where it was recovered, in relationship to where it should have went in, the condition of the body when it was recovered. Did it match what a body should look like at that amount of time in the water.

The position of the body, was it face down or on its back, and if the circumstances about that lividity—when the blood settles in the body after death—it takes anywhere from eight to 12 hours. We can tell that it's not consistent with the way the person drowned. And then there's taxonomy. What we have is the evidence that leads away from where the victims were going…

KING: Anthony, that makes the puzzlement even greater. So we have possibly many people going around killing people, putting a smiley face. Are they copycats, Anthony? What's your read? What's your theory?

DUARTE: Well, as Kevin said earlier, it's definitely not just the smiley face. We have different clusters in different parts of the country that are tied in. Smiley face is probably the least part of it…

KING: We reached out to the New York Police Department for an updated comment on Patrick McNeil's death and on the theories of former detectives Gannon and Duarte and we received no response…

It's a puzzlement. We'll have more in 60 seconds.

[COMMERCIAL BREAK > RETURN TO HOST]

KING: Kevin Gannon and Anthony Duarte, former New York PD detectives stay with us. Joining us from San Francisco is Candice Delong, former profiler for the FBI. We asked the FBI to comment on all this and what they told us, in essence, was they have not developed any evidence to support links between these tragic deaths. And that the vast majority appear to be alcohol-related drownings. Candice, what's your read?

CANDICE DELONG, FORMER FBI PROFILER: Well, the FBI's Behavioral Science Unit looked extensively at this, in addition to using their violent criminal apprehension program, which is a computerized tracking system. And they don't see any links. I don't know if the two New York detectives have met with the profiling unit or not. And unfortunately, it's sad but true. Now, notwithstanding the Patrick

McNeil case, sadly a lot of young people do die of accidental deaths, many times drowning, on our college campuses throughout the nation.

KING: Were you impressed with what Dr. Wecht had to say?

DELONG: Yes, regarding that particular case in New York, that certainly does sound like it was a homicide. I, however, fail to see the connection between the New York case and these other mid-western cases. Perhaps we could learn.

[CUT TO GANNON]

GANNON: We've looked at the work that the Behavioral Science Unit, the Behavioral Analysis Unit did in La Crosse, as well as the BCI, Bureau of Criminal Investigation from the state, along with the La Crosse detective bureau. When we looked at that work, in five of those cases, there was a lot of evidence that obviously was missed. In three of the cases, there's evidence leading away from where the police have—they all say they suspect the individuals came out of the bars, walked three blocks to the Mississippi River and floated in.

As my partner Anthony always says, if you don't want the answers, don't ask the question. And they brought these dogs in and the dogs led to the river and that was it. But when the dogs led them somewhere else after that, they disregarded the second part of the search, which to us is not doing a complete and open evaluation. And in two of the cases a living witness—we can prove that that living witness was held for five hours before put in the water, as attempted murder. And Lou Coleman was dead before he went into the water, clearly.

KING: Anthony, this must boggle your mind then, feelings that you have that you feel are murders and are not being taken seriously?

DUARTE: That's exactly right, Larry. You're born with certain instincts and gut feelings. And when you feel something that's not right, chances are it's really not right. And if you see something that's not right and you don't act upon it, in essence, you're actually sanctioning that type of action.

KING: How do you respond to that, Candice?

DELONG: Well, I agree that, certainly, instincts are important. I would simply like to point out that the FBI in cases like this, where they are consulted, any additional information that comes up will be taken into consideration and an additional assessment will be made. In this particular case, the FBI, they basically had three choices. Of course, now, I think we're looking at what, 25 to 30 deaths, but the choices would be: Yes, we agree that this is—these are murders of a serial nature. No, we totally disagree. Or this is inconclusive; we need more information, we cannot say. And they have come out and said they don't see any evidence of a serial nature.

KING: At this point—thanks, Candice. We'll come back and we'll talk to a gang specialist from a school where an alleged victim went missing. Stay with us.

[COMMERCIAL BREAK > RETURN TO HOST]

KING: Gannon and Duarte remain in New York. Joining us from Minneapolis is Dr. Lee Gilbertson. He's a gang specialist and associate professor, department of criminal justice studies at St. Cloud State Universities. He's been working with the detectives, examining possible linkages between the case. He got involved.

What, a student in your school was one of those found dead?

DR. LEE GILBERTSON, PROFESSOR OF CRIMINOLOGY AT ST. CLOUD UNIVERSITY: Yes, Larry, Scott Radel back in February of 2006.

KING: What were the circumstances?

GILBERTSON: Scott was downtown with his friends drinking and he became separated from them. And he was supposed to meet them in one direction at a bar but ended up going in the opposite direction. Later, he was found drowned in the Mississippi River.

KING: What are your thoughts? You heard the FBI specialist say that a lot of kids die of drowning every year.

GILBERTSON: Well, that's true, Larry. But if you actually look at the statistics on drownings, most drownings occur during the summer and they're related to water activities like boating and water skiing and things like that. Very few drownings actually occur during the winter. And those are generally associated with ice fishing and snowmobiling and things like that, up in our northern region.

When I looked at these cases, the first thing that jumped out at me was the victimological profile. It's not a normal distribution. You don't have tall fat people, or tall skinny people and short fat or skinny people. They're all right in the middle. The profile is very, very thin. The standard deviation is only 0.4 on their weight and height...

[CUT TO CROSSTALK & HOST]

KING: All right, go ahead.

GILBERTSON: I have spatial profiles across the United States as well as where they land within the city. Time, I've gotten really good at predicting the time. But it really distresses me that I can't pick the location. Evidentiary, Kevin alluded to it. In many of the cases, if you follow the trail where evidence was reintroduced into the scene after the search or dogs tracked them in one direction, between 150 and 180 degrees in the opposite direction is where you found the body. Symbolic is the next one—

KING: Because of time limitations, Doctor, I'm going to break it down to what do you believe is going on?

GILBERTSON: I believe, looking at these different patterns as they're put together, that we have a large group that operates under one ideology across the United States, broken up and working, operating—however you want to describe it—in separate cells under a schedule to commit these crimes.

KING: So it's a group of people in different parts of the country killing people, leaving that smiley face as an example. And there's a pattern to it and there's a common belief among the killers.

GILBERTSON: There is a common belief. And the fourth member of our team, Adam Carlson, that's his area. And he tells us it's actually homogenization of four political and religious beliefs...

KING: We're out of time. We're going to do a lot more on this. We thank Kevin Gannon, Anthony Duarte, Dr. Lee Gilbertson.

DUARTE: Thanks so much for having us.

[EXIT INTERVIEW]

"Kevin Gannon, the ex-New York cop who believes a team of 'smiley-face' serial killers is responsible for the drownings of young men across the country, was investigated in the sexual assault of a 19-year-old University of St. Thomas student last spring during the search for a missing St. Thomas freshman. The investigation was closed late last summer after Ramsey County prosecutors 'reviewed the case and declined charges citing insufficient evidence'...." *Saint Paul Pioneer Press, March 2010*

"I find it interesting that, while this assault case was closed last summer, the St. Paul Police Department found it necessary to call the media the day after I spoke with St. Paul Mayor Chris Coleman...similar to the 'leak' made to WCCO on Februrary 8th of my son's supposed issues with his sexuality...As for [Kevin Gannon] giving families false hope—what's more hopeless than having SPPD's Senior Commander tell you that 'your son was a very troubled young man, we'll find him when the river gives him up. We don 't have time to look for him'...!" *editorial rebuttal from Sally Zamlen, mother of 2009 drowning victim Dan Zamlen*

Chapter 12: Mud and a River

ST. PAUL, MINNESOTA - MAY 1, 2009: "The search for University of St. Thomas freshman Dan Zamlen ended today when his body was discovered in the Mississippi River near the Ford Motor plant. Zamlen went missing on April 5, 2009 after a night out with his classmates. Walking home he had called a friend and in the final seconds of their conversation had cried out for help before the phone went dead. Large volunteer teams and police with sonar, tracking dogs, and a helicopter searched the river bluffs and the water near the site, but there had been no signs of the 19-year-old until now. His body was found just before noon by a Ford employee who was at the water checking the plant's intake system. Zamlen was identified by items in his wallet, according to sources informed by the police. The St. Paul Police Department has not released any further details."

- - -

It's not a cheap proposition for any police force to investigate even just one questionable death, let alone a string of them. And before such an undertaking could ever be launched the price would have to be considered, not only from a financial aspect but also in terms of its toll on a municipality's reputation.

When the major source of that municipality's wealth and reputation—its very livelihood—is so dependent upon a local university and the uninterrupted flow of students to and from it annually, there's bound to be some balking by officials when it comes to acknowledging serial deaths within their boundaries. Even when the public has already taken notice of the problem and it's getting harder and harder to deny it. Even when the victims are mostly college students.

No doubt about it, investigations of that sort can be cost prohibitive.

That's why it took people by surprise when they learned the Saint Paul Police Department in Minnesota had devoted so much of their time and resources in 2010 to compiling a 400-page report on drowning victim Dan Zamlen's supposed homosexuality issues. The real reason, the SPPD suddenly insisted, for why he disappeared and ended up dead in the Mississippi River in spring of 2009.

Although originally ruling his death in 2009 as accidental, Zamlen's drowning was in reality "a suicide" the SPPD newly confided to reporters in 2010, publicly responding at long last to Sally Zamlen's constant pleas for them to reopen her son's case.

The young man was having some very serious angst about his sexuality, the police announced, and, as their 400-page press release clearly demonstrated, he took his own life because of it. "Case closed. No further comments."

Still, a glance at the circumstances of Zamlen's April 5th 2009 disappearance, and the results of the search for him and of his autopsy findings, would show ample enough reason for his death to have been labeled suspicious right from the very beginning. So it's completely understandable why a parent would have wanted the police to provide a more thorough probe than his case had received: It's understandable why it might've looked like foul play.

On the night Dan Zamlen vanished he had just left a downtown St. Paul bar in which he and a group of his classmates had been carousing until the early hours of morning. Reportedly he'd left that establishment sometime after 2:00 AM, alone because he'd had a few words with another patron and wanted to walk it all off, maybe meet up with some of his buddies at the neighboring University of Minnesota, if they were still awake and receiving visitors at that hour.

In fact, he was en route there, he'd just informed his friend, Anna, via a cellphone conversation on Mississippi Boulevard at Saint Claire. Obviously, though, Zamlen was somehow intercepted on his way because he never made it beyond that location—his last words to Anna being "Oh-my-god, help!"

Dan Zamlen was a responsible and caring individual; a straight A student, a Three-Star athlete, an Eagle Scout, a Catechism teacher, and a former altar boy. He had also recently diagnosed himself as a diabetic and was wearing an insulin pod the day of his disappearance which, whenever empty or submersed, would beep a loud warning signal intermittently for about a week until its energy pack was drained.

It was a lightweight, state-of-the-art delivery device and didn't require embedding beneath the skin, but it still had to be replenished every few days. Therefore

Zamlen's health was a pressing concern to his family and explained why they sped promptly to the scene upon learning he was officially missing.

Friends and family tried repeatedly to contact Zamlen after his last worrisome conversation, but they only got voicemail each time they tried to call him. The friend he'd spoken with before their conversation ended abruptly said she'd even driven to the particular intersection he told her he was calling from, but when she got there she said Zamlen was already gone.

The cellphone model Zamlen's parents had provided him with for college was a model that, as long it remained charged and fully operative would be trackable through GPS, if it should ever be necessary for them to have to do this. But, by 8:30 the very same morning, that cellphone had gone dead, with still no word from, or sign of, its owner. So a special GPS feature that should have provided a locational ping turned out to be worthless technology without the police actually bothering to track it right away.

The testimony of Dan Zamlen's friend, Anna, the last person he is alleged to have communicated with, would change many times in the telling and retelling of this story, making her multi-versions and possible embellishments of the original events a significant bone of contention for the Zamlen family members.

The Zamlens were only trying to determine what exactly had happened to their loved one that night, but, as a consequence of the young woman's unreliability, found her to be quite confounding and untrustworthy.

Nevertheless, the initial version is always what counts the most in these cases, and initially Anna had said that whatever spurred the dispute Zamlen was involved in that evening, which caused him to erupt and storm off by himself, it was relatively unimportant.

Regardless of what actually took place at the bar, minor or major, commonsense still dictates that if someone's last words before they disappeared were cries for help, then those concerned for the victim's welfare should have been able to enlist the aid of law enforcement to search for him without delay.

But when Zamlen went missing in April 2009 this was not yet how such matters were handled by the authorities. Instead, the Saint Paul Police Department advised his parents that they'd have to wait at least 24 hours before the youth could legally be considered a missing person. "Your son is a grown man," the police reminded them. "His lack of contact doesn't rise to the level of concern as a missing child."

Naturally, it goes without saying, if a male or female of any age has met up with some type of misfortune, an awful lot can happen in only 24 hours to deepen the tragedy. And, apparently, an awful lot did.

The SSPD did not join the civilian rescue efforts which were spearheaded by Zamlen's loved ones and launched immediately upon their arrival in the city of Saint Paul. Worse, police tried to prevent the search for him, the Zamlens said, expressly forbidding them from walking down the rocky bluffs near where their son was last heard from, and even stationing an officer in the area with the aim of discouraging anyone else from scaling them.

Those bluffs were just "too dangerous," the SSPD told would-be rescuers. A warning the searchers felt compelled to disobey.

So it would be more than two days of their fruitlessly combing the location and knocking door-to-door throughout the neighborhood before the distraught Zamlens actually got to meet with a missing persons investigator; and when police finally did look for Dan Zamlen, all eight bloodhounds they employed followed the victim's scent away from the river toward yet another intersection where the scent then faded.

The SPPD scoured the perilous bluffs themselves, too, but they also found no evidence of anyone having accidentally tumbled over and down onto the shore below. The rocks, the trees and the soil of these several story high embankments being completely undisturbed.

Sophisticated side-sonar scanning of the river and infrared technology likewise produced no corpse hidden in the frigid murk of the Mississippi, and the same was true for searching by air from police helicopters equipped with thermal tracking capabilities who also spotted nothing in or around the water.

But by then this news wasn't a big surprise to the Zamlen posse, numbering about 1200 strong and comprised of family members, friends, fellow university students, and one ex-NYPD detective who suspected foul play and a link with similar cases he'd been investigating. In all, the Zamlen search party had knocked on 7000 doors to find the missing young man and, sadly, had come up empty-handed.

"We looked in the culverts, we looked in the trees," Dan Zamlen's father declared in exasperation. "I don't really believe he's in the river."

Having pretty much drawn the same conclusion, the Saint Paul Police Department terminated their own efforts after only three days of hunting for the victim. When, almost a month later, Dan Zamlen's body was finally pulled out of the river a few miles downstream at the Ford Motor plant, they officially ruled it a drowning from a drunken fall and closed the case soon thereafter when the autopsy results came in showing no signs of physical trauma.

Dissatisfied and still hoping they might find important clues, the Zamlen's continued looking for their son's cellphone, but never found it. They discovered instead a smiley face with horns spray-painted on a sign at Ford Motors, and yet another sketched onto a baseball which was left in the vicinity Zamlen had first disappeared.

Neither item was relevant to his case, the Saint Paul police then insisted, at this point in time far more interested in investigating the sex abuse allegations against Kevin Gannon which had recently surfaced, than in entertaining the Smiley Face Murder theory the detective was now so famous for espousing.

The results of a second autopsy on Zamlen didn't sway them an inch from this new course they'd chosen either, in spite of the second medical examiner's concerns that the corpse wasn't displaying any injuries from falling down the rocky and brush-filled bluffs where the SPPD claimed he did.

"It is likely he drowned," examiner number two affirmed, "but I feel the manner of death cannot be determined and requires more police investigation and/or access to existing police records."

Of course, the doctor wasn't referring to 400-plus pages discussing adnauseum the victim's sexuality...

Anger can be a powerful coping mechanism in times of grief and the heartbroken Zamlen family had plenty of reason to be angry with the SSPD's treatment of their son's case, both before and after his body was located, and ever since.

"There are a lot of upset people here right now over the disrespecting of my son and his good name," the victim's mother said. She denounced the SPPD's campaign to paint her son out as a confused, suicidal homosexual, and Kevin Gannon as a dangerous sexual predator, as nothing but a ruse and a cover up.

"I don't believe any investigation was really done," Mrs. Zamlen stated emphatically. "I'm through with the police. They've done nothing for me, and I feel sorry for the taxpayers in Saint Paul."

She continues today to try and piece all the evidence together on her own, she said.

As to what really did happen to Dan Zamlen on April 5th 2009 which somehow led to his entering the Mississippi River and supposedly drowning, "We don't know," a spokesman for the Saint Paul Police Department admitted. "And we may never know," he added dismissively. "But barring any new evidence and information, the investigation is complete and inactive."

"They're making my brother seem like a drunken jerk who fell over the railing into the river," Victoria Hart said.

"My son did not fall in that river," Gregory Hart's father insisted. "Those marks on my son's face—somebody hit him."

Hart's family said, when they went to the Providence police about his disappearance, they were told "get lost and file the report in Boston."

Hart's grandfather also claimed that even before it was known his grandson was dead and his body discovered in the Woonasquatucket River, the police had stated "he probably got drunk and drowned."

Chapter 13: Signs of Foul Play

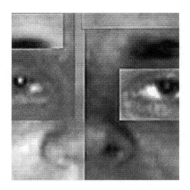

PROVIDENCE, RHODE ISLAND - MARCH 23, 2010: "The body of Gregory Hart, 23, of Dedham Massachusetts, was found in the Woonasquatucket River late Tuesday afternoon. Police say the UMass economics graduate and certified scuba diver was 'highly intoxicated' and drowned to death in the river.

Hart disappeared late Saturday evening from the Red Room Bar in Providence which is owned by the wife of a Providence police detective. The victim's body was discovered in the river by family and friends who say he looked beaten not drowned. His eye socket had been severely damaged, his clothes torn, and there were cuts on his knuckles and cheek."

- - -

Just prior to 23-year-old Gregory Hart's disappearance from a Providence Rhode Island pub at 1:30 in the morning of March 14th 2010, local law enforcement officials in that town had made the national news for charges of conspiracy and corruption. From the ongoing "Operation Deception" bust of the Providence Police Department's cocaine ring, which had already led to a half dozen arrests of crooked cops, to the matter of a Providence police detective having been charged with assault and battery after being videotaped beating a handcuffed man with a flashlight, the PPD was hip deep in scandal.

Further undermining confidence in their handling of the out-of-towner's disappearance and drowning death was that the investigating officer just happened to be the husband to the Red Room's owner, the bar Hart had vanished from. This conflict, and the PPD's assertion the victim fell into the water at a location which would have necessitated his scaling a tall cement wall *and* the eight-foot fence atop it to get to the riverbank (acrobatic feats accomplished with a BAC allegedly three times the legal driving limit). also raised a number of serious doubts.

The PPD's failure to launch a search for Hart when his family first reported his disappearance to them didn't help matters either. Nor did the discovery of missing video from the bar's interior and exterior surveillance cameras recorded on that evening…and the bar bouncer immediately leaving town before he could be questioned…and other important eyewitnesses—friends of Hart who had been with him all night—suddenly clamming up and even declining to join the volunteer search-and-rescue teams out looking for him.

Everything about the case was odd from the start.

"When a sudden death happens in an unusual place under unusual circumstances, it's suspicious," Major Thomas F. Oates from the Providence Police Department announced when Greg Hart's body was retrieved from the nearby Woonasquatucket River on March 16th 2011.

The commanding investigator of the Hart case, Officer Oates was attempting to quell rumors already circulating about a possible police cover up regarding a disturbance or altercation at the bar the victim was last seen alive in. On this score, reframing the public's low opinion of the police department, the Major wasn't meeting with too much success, however. Mostly because of the battered condition of the corpse.

In March of 2010, the Woonasquatucket River was roiling from a spring melt and heavy rains, its raging waters almost overflowing Providence's riverbanks. That means it wasn't impossible, if someone did accidentally fall in someplace with no one close by to see or hear them struggling, even if they were an expert swimmer and a licensed scuba diver like Hart was, they might still be overcome by the fast and freezing cold currents and drown.

And, if they did die in rushing waters, their body might also sustain a broken jaw and a shattered eye socket, some scrapes on their knuckles and bruises on their shins.

Of course, it's also reasonable to expect they'd have the same amount of injuries on the back of their body too, since, after all, they are being tossed about and pummeled against the rocks, with other floating objects, indiscriminately.

But Hart's body didn't. Only the front of him was damaged.

Although the Providence police claimed they found no evidence of the victim having been in a fight that evening, the truth is they had just issued a report of an altercation at the bar only slightly before Hart went missing. Other reports the police initially made would also change dramatically as the investigation continued.

For instance, the PPD originally stated they'd recovered Hart's cellphone in the parking lot outside the Red Room. But when the Hart family went to claim it in hopes of deciphering his last messages, the police report had been altered. It then read that the cellphone had been on Hart's person the entire three days he was in the water.

Moreover, when the victim's family demanded the Providence Police Department release the cellphone to them so they could access its records, the PPD finally handed it over *in five broken pieces*, asserting that even the Rhode Island State Police had been unable to retrieve information from it in that decimated condition.

"This phone definitely wasn't in the water," a data recovery specialist for TechFusion exclaimed when the Harts brought it to the company for his analysis. "Definitely, 100 percent, this was not in the water," he assured them.

Techfusion's expert knew this because the particular Apple iPhone model Greg Hart owned came with a discreet feature in it, tiny indicators that, for warranty purposes, would signal if the phone had been submerged in liquid or spilled on, thus voiding the company's product liability in a replacement claim.

These hidden sensors were nearly impossible to remove evidently, but on Hart's phone they had been intentionally scratched off, the specialist reported.

Coincidentally, while the cellphone appeared to have never been in the water, according to those who'd first examined the victim's body at the riverside, he hadn't been submerged for very long, either. By all descriptions, certainly not for the entire length of time he'd been missing.

In fact, Hart's father had already suspected as much, noting that only the fingertips of his son actually looked wrinkled at the time he'd been recovered from the river. Three to five hours or half a day was the best estimation. Although where the victim could have been before that time nobody had a clue.

The Rhode Island medical examiner ruled Gregory Hart's death an accidental drowning on March 23rd 2011, but never released the toxicology findings. However, Providence police later informed the Harts that their son had been extremely inebriated when he died, with a blood/alcohol level three times over the legal limit for operating a motor vehicle.

There is, unfortunately, no way to confirm or deny this.

Some people, such as the officers from the Providence Police Department, might say that young men like Gregory Hart have been reaping the ill consequences of too much drink ever since public taverns were first created. But one could also reasonably argue: how does a man learn to hold his liquor if he never loses control of the reins?

In either case, regardless of moral beliefs, no one should expect to die when merely out celebrating a new job with their friends. Not in the 21st century.

The Hart family is still seeking answers and justice for the death of their loved one, and are offering a $70,000 reward for any information that would lead to the arrest and conviction of the party or parties responsible for his suspicious disappearance and drowning. To learn more about Gregory Hart and to view the reward terms visit www.JusticeforGregHart.com.

"I miss my son every day," Marianne Hart said in a recent 2012 interview. "I won't give up on Greg,'' she promised. "There are people who know what happened to him that night. We will find out. No matter how long it takes.''

Chapter 14: Profile of a Serial Murderer

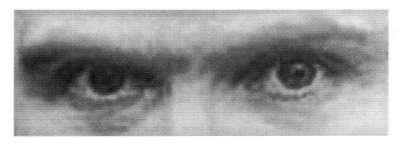

You might like to think that, if you happened to glance into those scary peepers pictured above, you'd know immediately to walk (or run) in the opposite direction, but this prolific serial killer fooled many of his victims into doing otherwise.

Armed with a smile and often sporting a crutch or a cast so he'd appear helpless, Ted Bundy confessed to battering, raping, torturing and then killing nearly three dozen college age women in approximately a fifteen-year period, taking credit for the last one on that list as he was being marched to the electric chair.

Truth is, the self-proclaimed "most cold-hearted sonofabitch you'll ever meet," whose own defense attorney described as "the very definition of heartless evil," deceived everybody he came in contact with. Even famed criminologist and bestselling author Ann Rule, who personally knew Bundy, didn't suspect her charismatic associate until officials began compiling a first-of-its-kind database in an effort to pinpoint similarities from what few clues existed about an elusive killer slaughtering attractive young females across the Pacific Northwest.

A sadistic predator who derived profound sexual pleasure from "possessing" and abusing his prey while they were still alive *and after their deaths*, Bundy was the quintessential serial murderer, matching this criminal profile in every possible way. It's also noteworthy to the current analysis that he too admitted to drowning at least one or more of his young victims.

It took nearly ten years after Bundy was put to death for a federal law to be enacted by the United States Congress which would, once and for all, attempt to provide a legal definition of serial murder. Titled the *Protection of Children from Sexual Predator Act of 1998* it formally defined serial homicide as a series of three or more killings sharing common characteristics such as would imply they were committed by the same person or persons.

These included the following stringent criteria:

- one or more offenders

- two or more victims

- distinctly separate events at different times

- a cooling off period between incidents

The FBI itself identifies serial murder as "the unlawful killing of two or more victims by the same offender(s), in separate events." What's more, in order to be officially considered a full-fledged serial murderer by the Bureau, one would have to commit at least three such homicides within a thirty-day period.

There is more than ample indication that serial killers have existed throughout time, but historians generally agree it was LAPD detective Pierce Brooks who first coined the term in the 1970's. That being said, although serial killing appears a popular activity these days when viewed through the Hollywood blockbuster lens, according to the FBI and other crime experts, serialized slayings do not amount to even one percent of all homicides committed annually.

What FBI statistics can unequivocally confirm, however, is the popular notion that serial killers are mainly young men—over 90% are males from 25 to 35 years of age. But it is fast becoming pure myth that these are exclusively Caucasians, as many experts are now suggesting that other races are simply being under-reported because they are perceived by a biased public and press as "not smart enough" to plan and perpetrate serial murders successfully. Adding to this widespread misperception, authorities say, is the over-sensationalizing of white male serial murderers in the media because their victims are, almost without exception, young and attractive females.

Regardless of race, ethnicity or sex, The FBI's *Crime Classification Manual* divides serial killers into three basic categories: *organized*, *disorganized* and *mixed*, the latter classification reserved for those who exhibit a blend of both organized and disorganized characteristics. (For example, some organized killers gradually descend into disorganized killings as they amass more and more victims.)

Hollywood's penchant for portraying these offenders as possessing devious brilliance in all aspects of their existence, and the public's willing belief in the same, is also perpetuating a fallacy. With only a mean IQ of 113 for the "organized" brand of serial killer, that's just slightly above an average intelligence, not by any means the kind of wiles considered to be at a genius level of, say, the Hannibal Lecter variety.

Organized serial murderers do plot their crimes intelligently, though, skillfully killing in one place and then dumping the body in another. Clever ploys like Bundy's crutches, leg casts, and arm slings are also fairly typical means of luring a victim too, but this type of killer proves just as opportunistic as any other criminal when on the prowl, selecting the most vulnerable members of society to murder, such as drifters or the homeless or prostitutes, whenever their ideal target escapes their grips.

But, whether it's an unsuspecting young woman or a luckless down-and-out, whomever they ultimately choose, control is the key word for individuals who fall under this particular classification. That is at the root of their deranged behavior—the desire to power.

In that same vein, it's not unusual for organized killers to acquire a replete understanding of forensic science and procedures so, once they've finished the grisly job they set out to accomplish, they can competently manipulate the crime scene and the corpse to hide their own tracks, eluding law enforcement officers while at the same time operating in plain sight of them.

Despite such painstaking efforts to avoid getting captured, these organized types are also the kind who take a great deal of pride in their "handiwork" and therefore crave and court attention to it with taunting notes and graffiti, some even boldly arranging victims' bodies in certain poses as a sort of recognizable signature. Strange as that may sound, many such a killer has overtly sought glory in this way, perhaps, in sending their gloating messages to reporters and the police, paying homage to, and mimicking, a much more famous predecessor:

"Dear Boss, I keep on hearing the police have caught me but they wont fix me just yet. I have laughed when they look so clever and talk about being on the right track. That joke about Leather Apron gave me real fits. I am down on whores and I shant quit ripping them till I do get buckled. Grand work the last job was. I gave the lady no time to squeal. How can they catch me now. I love my work and want to start again. You will soon hear of me with my funny little games. I saved some of the proper red stuff in a ginger beer bottle over the last job to write with but it went thick like glue and I cant use it. Red ink is fit enough I hope ha. ha. The next job I do I shall clip the ladys ears off and send to the police officers just for jolly wouldn't you. Keep this letter back till I do a bit more work, then give it out straight. My knife's so nice and sharp I want to get to work right away if I get a chance. Good luck.

— Yours truly, Jack the Ripper"

Not quite as antisocial as his more disorganized counterparts, an organized serial slayer, when finally identified and brought to justice, almost always manages to shock the neighborhood he resides in, as well as his loved ones, colleagues, and closest friends. None of whom could have ever guessed in a million years that such a "nice" guy would be capable of performing such atrocities.

Disorganized serial killers, on the other hand, don't tend to generate that big a surprise once they're actually apprehended. Having a mean IQ of only 92.5 which, on the intelligence spectrum, rates somewhat below average, these are usually social misfits who display far more palpable warning signs of mental aberrations. This category of serial murder kills impulsively as the urge and opportunity strikes, and does so in a characteristically brutal manner with whatever weapon is available to them at the time. Extreme sexual violence, necrophilia, cannibalism, and in some cases skinning their victims (as with the Ed Gein murders, aka the "Texas Chainsaw Massacre"), these bizarre acts are the norm and not the exception for this particular class of offender.

As to murder motives in general, aside from obvious mental disease and deeply disturbed thinking, all three classifications of serial killers have cited a host of prompts for their repeat offenses. These have been seen to overlap in many cases, particularly where organized and disorganized traits have merged, but they generally fall under the following separate categories:

1. Visionary (e.g. hearing voices, etc.)
2. Mission Oriented, (e.g. religion-based or purging of "undesirables", etc.)
3. Hedonistic (subsets of which include Lust, Thrill, and Comfort)
4. Power/Control. ("achieving" greatness/dominance by brutalizing others)

While most of the male killers will claim to have acted upon any or all of those four incentives, or various combinations of them, hedonistic "comfort killing" is chiefly the domain of the roughly five-percent minority of serial murderers who have yet to be discussed in any detail here. Namely females who routinely kill with the object of inheriting from the deceased certain things of monetary value, like life insurance benefits, investment accounts, real estate, and other forms of transferrable property. Homicides of this nature require psychological cunning over physical cruelty in order to be executed successfully and, thus, are done with very little zeal and bloodshed— fast acting poison being the weapon of choice, usually. And sometimes drowning.

"There is no evidence of victim trauma…in one death (Patrick McNeill) this is evident, but he was deceased prior to entering the water and did not drown."

"The supposition that only males are drowning does not necessarily support a serial killer theory."

The Center For Homicide Research, in their 2010 study attempting to debunk the Smiley Face Murder theory

Chapter 15: Sinking Fears

TABLE. Estimated annual number*, percentage, and rate[†] of persons treated in emergency departments for nonfatal recreation-related and fatal recreation-related drownings[§], by selected characteristics — United States, 2001–2002   Center for Disease Control

Characteristic	Nonfatal				Fatal			
	Estimated no.	(%)	Rate	(95% CI¶)	No.	(%)	Rate	(95% CI)
Age (yrs)								
0–4	2,168**	(52.0)	11.13	(3.56–18.69)	442	(13.1)	2.28	(2.07–2.50)
5–14	1,058	(25.3)	2.58	(1.13–4.02)	333	(9.9)	0.81	(0.72–0.90)
≥15	948	(22.7)	0.42	(0.20–0.64)	2,563	(76.0)	1.14	(1.10–1.18)
Unknown	—	—	—	—	34	(1.0)	—	—
Sex								
Male	2,721	(65.2)	1.93	(1.16–2.70)	2,789	(82.7)	1.99	(1.92–2.06)
Female	1,452††	(34.8)	1.00	(0.27–1.72)	583	(17.3)	0.40	(0.37–0.43)
Location								
Pool	2,751	(65.9)	0.96	(0.40–1.51)	596	(17.7)	0.21	(0.19–0.23)
Natural water	909	(21.8)	0.32	(0.14–0.49)	1,467	(43.5)	0.51	(0.49–0.54)
Other/Unspecified	513	(12.3)	—	—	1,309	(38.8)	—	—
Disposition								
Treated and released	1,925	(46.1)	0.67	(0.29–1.05)	—	—	—	—
Hospitalized/Transferred	2,233	(53.5)	0.78	(0.44–1.12)	—	—	—	—
Other/Unknown	16	(0.4)	—	—	—	—	—	—
Total	4,174	(100.0)	1.46	(0.77–2.14)	3,372	(100.0)	1.18	(1.14–1.22)

* Numbers might not add to totals because of rounding. † Per 100,000 ¶ Confidence interval. § Data for fatal recreation-related drownings are for 2001

** Although this estimate is based on 119 cases, it might be unstable. The coefficient of variation is 35% because of an over-representation of children treated in National Electronic Injury Surveillance System All Injury Program (NEISS-AIP) children's hospitals, affecting the variance of the estimate.

†† Although this estimate is based on 71 cases, it might be unstable. The coefficient of variation is 37% because small NEISS-AIP hospitals are under-represented in this subgroup, affecting the variance of the estimate.

Center For Disease Control: tables for recreational drowning deaths and incidents for 2004

The theory has become a bit convoluted of late, but the actual gravamen of the interstate killer allegation is that certain types of young males living within close range of certain northern U.S. highways are being murdered *somehow* and their corpses later placed in nearby bodies of water *to appear* as if they accidentally drowned. NOT that they are being slain through the act of drowning itself.

It's a fearful people who think such fearsome thoughts, granted, but this desperate theorizing isn't really that farfetched when viewed from a forensic perspective. Because, whether by drowning or asphyxiation through another means, the result could look the same in a basic autopsy—a drowning victim's lungs don't necessarily fill with water.

In fact, experts say many victims drown with little or no water ever entering their lungs. MedAire/MedLink's drown-specialist explains, "Most often there is a small amount of water inhaled and an involuntary spasm of the epiglottis that prevents the lungs from being completely filled."

This natural response to submersion is called laryngospasm and when fully triggered will produce a "dry drowning" event as opposed to a "wet" one. According to RescueDiver.org, laryngospasm is, to some extent, common in all types of drowning deaths. That involuntary reflex is also the reason why a person in the throes of drowning are unable to call out for help, since they can't do so without air.

As to the relatively recent fascination with smiley faces and their anonymous artisans, this flamboyant iconography is secondary to the overriding precept of a cleverly crafted "accident", for the simple reason that, even before attention was called to its possible connection, citizens never had to rely on the presence of graffiti at the water's edge to justify their supposition of foul play. They needed only to point to the disproportionately high number of non-recreational cold weather "drownings" occurring in their region over the past fifteen years.

Serial killing is a popular topic these days, standard fare in our movies and novels and video games. But, due to the association in the present case with a universally recognized symbol, it's become the otherwise minor smiley face aspect of the I-90 and I-94 murder theory that has garnered the most media attention, unfortunately.

Typically, it's useful to obtain national exposure for an issue that's been deliberately marginalized, swept under the rug by local police and politicians. Except this kind of sensationalism seems to have put a somewhat silly spin on the whole matter. To the point of seriously distracting from what area residents and their spokespeople are actually trying to say.

Thus, the playful novelty of a smiling face, while broadly appealing, has only served to obfuscate instead of illuminate a life-threatening situation.

This then will help to explain why, in 2010, when the Center For Homicide Research published a study titled "Drowning the Smiley Face Murder Theory" they also misconstrued the public's belief about these disappearances and deaths; singularly and erroneously focusing their research on flouncing the idea of murder-by-drowning and the so called smiley face serial killers' hallmark happy signature, as opposed to analyzing the actual facts and statistics.

Another costly public relations stunt, another swipe at the theorists, another missed opportunity. And more unnecessary fatalities, as a result of the standoff.

Although the issue of whether water can be used as a weapon of death is not dispositive and it neither advances nor defeats the original theory to argue that it can't, I think it's important to scrutinize CHR's publicized findings here anyway.

Why is it relevant if it's irrelevant? Because the research is greatly flawed, and yet CHR's study delivered such a crushing blow to the theory's chief proponents, outright admonishing them and their followers for "observational bias" and "group think", that it effectively silenced all meaningful public discussion about the drownings ever since.

Designed with the obvious agenda of debunking for good the idea of a gang of murderers on a fifteen-year drowning spree in the northern corridor, the Center for Homicide Research lambasted the serial murder theory. But utilizing a so called "non-recreational outdoor drowning database" to support their various findings, while tacitly admitting that this crucial database was "problematic" because "it has some shortcomings in the form of missing data," is just the first of many pitfalls in their argument.

The second is that it's not known which "non-recreational" drowning database CHR was actually referring to in their paper since, oddly enough, they don't bother to name it. Neither do they say if the cases listed in it were independently compiled by a recognized authority and whether the statistic gathering was international or domestic.

They do say on page two of their study that "CHR identified an Internet database of 40 water-related deaths and have continued adding cases to it." A perplexingly vague statement which raises the possibility that, aside from a handful of online lists maintained *unofficially* by some conscientious individuals, the database CHR was alluding to doesn't really exist.

In either case, because researchers "adding cases" to reinvent an existing database that will, once modified, support their research conclusions, is rather an unusual and unscholarly approach to fact-finding, this admission piqued my curiosity.

So I conducted a sweeping search to see if I could locate the Homicide Center's top secret source myself, but, regrettably, and as might have been expected, I could not.

In fact, even today there isn't an authoritative database that I know of dedicated to compiling non-recreational outdoor drowning statistics, let alone for the specific months of September to April in the northern USA, since, as it turns out, such events don't happen very often. The chart I provided on water fatalities in this chapter was the closest I could find on the subject and was generated by The Center For Disease Control in the year 2004. But as you can see in a glance, this one concerns both drowning and near-drowning events which happen in recreational settings. Moreover, it's not all that recent, representing data the CDC collected from 2001 to 2002.

Still, when analyzing those figures, recreational drownings are surprisingly low when one takes into consideration the countless millions of Americans who swim and boat each year. In fact, with recreational drowning listed by the CDC as only "the seventh leading cause of unintentional-injury deaths *for all ages*" it would seem that playing in water or near it, sober or intoxicated, isn't quite the dangerous act some experts are now claiming it to be.

CDC also states the findings for this period to be consistent with their previous reports showing "small children are at the highest risk" of death by drowning, "particularly around residential pools," they warn. Fatal drowning rates for the male population were noted to be "five times that of females" by CDC estimates, although the organization offered no definitive explanation for that latter ratio.

Which means, we can hypothesize all we want about it, but so far no one can really say why it is that more men than women die during water recreation. And, at this rate, if we don't keep probing for the answers, we may never find out why *only* young males are dying in non-recreational drownings around the northern interstates.

The Center For Homicide Research emphatically asserts "there is no known serial offender who has ever drowned victims." Again, this is not only an off topic statement, but it's also false. Both Coral Watts and Ted Bundy specifically employed drowning as one of their murder methods.

Additionally, although female serial murderers are still a rare phenomena even in today's violent times, a few such women as well have calculatingly used water to kill. Indeed, as CHR must have known, or should have known, the record shows a full five percent of all female serial killers' victims were intentionally drowned to death.

In trying to give a line by line analysis of CHR's "Drowning the Smiley Face Murder Theory" it was a repeated hindrance not being able to refer to a bona fide database for non-recreational drowning. Even the one CHR alleges to have banged together for their private use would've been handy so we could checkout their math. Math matters in research and it's not inconsequential that they omitted it, however, there are plenty of other assertions they made that appear equally skewed which can quickly be compared.

For instance, CHR spottily relied upon the Center for Disease Control's 2005 "Death and Dying" statistics which cite accidents as the number one cause of death in males and females 15 to 24 years of age, and suicides as the third leading cause of death in this demographic:

"Many of these drowning victims appear to be drinking to the point of total inebriation," CHR elaborates on page five of their paper. "Binge drinking is a strong predictor of actual suicide attempts."

Naturally, suicide being that prevalent in the young, the Homicide Center hoped the figure would bolster their position that many of the winter drownings were actually the result of auto-assassination, or, more plainly put, the fulfillment of a subconscious death wish.

Writing these off as merely due to death wishes, though, is much too convenient, since virtually none of the young men who went missing and ended up drowned ever expressed suicidal ideations to anyone. More importantly, in pursuit of this type of conjecture, which was at the expense of the victims' reputations, CHR entirely failed to mention the number two cause of death listed by the CDC for that age group: Homicide.

According to the Center for Disease Control, homicide is the second leading cause of death in Americans 15 to 24 years of age, accounting nationwide for over 16% of all fatalities in this particular segment of the population, and with males being six times more likely to be murdered than their female counterparts.

I'll reiterate that stat because it's pertinent and being deliberately ignored: The second leading cause of death in young men is homicide, not drowning.

Noteworthy too, the CDC's "Death and Dying" stats for the year 2010 indicated the data they collected for this period was totally "stable" with findings from previous years dating all the way back to 1997 when the first questionable drowning of Patrick McNeill occurred.

The only prominent statistical deviation being *a steady decline in suicides*.

Finally, it's important to note at least a decade's worth of CDC studies consistently show that nearly all accidental deaths in the 15 to 24 age bracket are caused by motor vehicle mishaps, not water. Recreational drowning deaths are included under this category, of course, because they do occur once in awhile, but these fall very, very low on the list. And non-recreational drownings, as I've already demonstrated, were completely off the CDC's radar.

Because of the those gaps in the logic and science of CHR's "Drowning the Smiley Face Murder Theory" study, there is no practical reason to debate each and every issue they've enumerated in it. Notwithstanding, and for those readers who may still be curious, the objections they made are listed verbatim next, stripped of the accompanying arguments but briefly summarized.

The twelve-page research document itself is copyrighted and therefore could not be reproduced in its entirety here, but a complete copy of CHR's analysis of this case is available for free download via their official website, a link to which can be found in this publication's resource index in the last section.

CENTER FOR HOMICIDE RESEARCH – 2010 [SYNOPSIS]
"DROWNING THE SMILEY FACE MURDER THEORY"

1. "There is a problem of time order." [the Center is implying there is no classic "cooling off period" between killings, a required showing per established serial murdering patterns, and that sometimes two or more "drownings" are occurring on the same day throughout the corridor]

2. "Graffiti is omnipresent." [since its advent in the 1960's, smiley faces are found everywhere in the world, even online]

3. "None of the smiley faces exactly match one another." [different artisans would suggest an organized group of murderers—traditionally, serial killers don't work in teams]

4. "The word 'Sinsiniwa' is a red herring." [this was found at one drowning site and seemed to reference the street name where another victim was later discovered, but this graffiti was not repeated often enough to establish a perceivable pattern, and the Native American word meaning "home of the young eagle" or "rattlesnake" is geographically commonplace]

5. "No criteria has been established specifying the necessary distance that a smiley face must occur in proximity to a deceased body in order to be counted."

6. "There is no evidence of victim trauma…in one death (Patrick McNeill) this was present, but he was deceased prior to entering the water and did not drown." [Center asserts murder must leave a mark]

7. "Homicidal drowning is extremely rare." [less than 1000 over a 21 year period – the Center estimates the portion of that total which were actually college-age victims to be approximately 117]

8. "The idea that water washes away evidence is a myth." [if a body is recovered from water quickly enough, sometimes evidence like blood and fibers "when correctly processed" can be lifted from it]

9. "The drownings don't fit a serial killer motif." [serial murders kill one at a time; employ torture, sexual assault and mutilation; select easy prey like women and children; rest between kills]

10. "Confessions by correction inmates are unreliable." [purportedly a prisoner bragged to a cellmate that he took part in the Jenkins crime; this case has since been reclassified a homicide]

11. "The general environment[s] of these disappearances are conducive to accidental drowning." [nighttime in Great Lakes region, as opposed to a well-lit desert - *also see #18]

12. "The supposition that only males are drowning does not necessarily support a serial killer theory." [serial murderers don't target strong young men - more males drown than females do]

13. "La Crosse Wisconsin foot patrols and police [allege they] have stopped over 50 intoxicated persons (fall 2006 through February 2010) from approaching the river late at night."

14. "The process by which intoxicated men accidentally fall into the river is already known and well-documented." [the Center "documented" some "footwear slipmarks on the riverbank in Minneapolis"]

15. "Many of the drowning cases are likely to have involved aspects of auto-assassination." [the Center is implying that the victims had a risky lifestyle and didn't consciously know they really wanted to kill themselves at the time they allegedly drowned]

16. "Malicious drugging of victims is unsupportable by the evidence." [a number of victims' autopsy reports showed elevated levels of GBH in their systems; GBH is an easily manufactured or obtained date-rape drug – the Center finds the drugging contention "untested and untestable"]

17. Presence of GBH (gamma-hydroxybutyric acid) in the victims' bodies does not indicate whether these victims were maliciously drugged or they knowingly administered the substance themselves." [also, but not noted by the Center: miniscule levels of GBH are produced through decomposition]

18. "The drowning of college students is not limited by region, but by climate." [in example, the Center says it found no such drownings in arid U.S. states like Arizona, Utah and Nevada due to "their absence of water" but allegedly did in the UK and Canada]

The Center For Homicide Research concludes its harsh, twelve-page rebuke of the Smiley Face Murder theory by expressing extreme frustration with the public's unwavering belief in it. They credited this to the theory's persuasive "central authority" veteran detective Kevin Gannon, claiming this "highly decorated and well-seasoned lead homicide investigator from the largest city in the United States" has blinded followers with his impressive credentials.

What the Center didn't explain is whether they found any evidence that would suggest Gannon makes a habit of doing such things, and, frankly, I couldn't find any proof that he does either.

As a matter of fact, this appears to be the only case the detective has ever so publicly pursued in this manner. The Smiley Face "conspiracy theory" is the one, and only one, Kevin Gannon has ever promulgated.

The Center's assertion is odder still because investigator Gannon and his team of experts made it more than abundantly clear in their 2008 CNN live interview that the linkage in these cross-country cases did not solely depend on smiley face graffiti; that the cases themselves did not involve genuine drownings, and that there was plenty of other evidence that necessarily had to be kept close to the chest for fear of copycats marring an ongoing investigation.

As well, the parents of the victims have also repeatedly stated they do not believe their sons died by drowning in lakes and rivers. Many have routinely conveyed this belief to the authorities and in the media, saying over and over and over again that their sons were killed in an unknown manner *elsewhere* and then dumped into the water at a much later date, their carefully deposited corpses to be discovered sometimes days, sometimes weeks, sometimes months, sometimes never.

So, unless it's an intentional mix up, unless the Homicide Center really didn't want to do its homework here, I cannot understand why it chose to obsessively devote all of its time and efforts to debunking the least important features of the theory, leaving the most salient ones outstanding.

Muddling through the grossly insensitive showmanship presented in "Drowning the Smiley Face Serial Theory" only one concrete fact stands out in it for certain: It doesn't matter how many, or who, believe that something strange and awful is going on in the northland, or how much evidence is submitted to support that contention, authorities like CHR, with their collective mindset, will never acknowledge that something is happening.

With blinkers fastened tight, the Center For Homicide Research officiously declares there is no serial killer on the loose here, and that is to be the end of the discussion, they hope. In this aspiration, their attitude is contemptuous and unyielding, and their work unforgivably shoddy and callous.

Nevertheless, I have to agree with them. These aren't the work of a serial murderer...

~~MISSING~~ DROWNED
cases examined for this report

Patrick, Richard, Charles, Anthony, Ryan, Larry, Nathan, Trevor, Joshua, Robert, Jeff, Brian, Chad, Patrick, Manuel, Ken, Justin, Branson, Eric, Chris, James, Lon, Craig, Chris, Michael, Nathan, Jeremy, Glenn, Matthew, Jared, Marlon, Kevin, Chris, Jesse, Adam, Christopher, Keith, Desmond, Pat, Dan, Frank, Josh, Todd, Patrick, Matt, Buddy, Albert, Matthew, Kenji, Scott, Max, Luke, Wade, Joseph, Nick, Dustin, Joshua, Abel, John, Chris, Josh, Matt, Tommy, Nicholas, Jeffrey, Willie, Eric, Trevor, Dan, Rian, Bill, Justin, Brendan, Ryan, William, Hyeong, Isaac, Brad, Russell, Sylvester, Jon, Craig, Gene, Jay, Rydell, Greg, Matt, Josh, James, Dwight, Nathan, Joe, Maurice, Jeremy, Devon, Willie, Timothy, Alan, Dave, Alex, George, Mark, Jeremy, Alexander, Ricky, Michael, James, Mike, Eric, Marcus, Tom, Damien, Franco, Lance, Jonathan, Brian, Samuel, Jesse, Nathan…

Chapter 16: Profile of a Mass Murderer

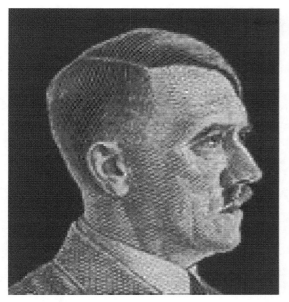

While serial murder finally has a legislated meaning, the term "mass murder" as yet has no formalized legal definition. But here in the United States both the Bureau of Justice Statistics and the FBI define it as four or more murders occurring during a specific event with no cooling-off period in between. The requirement of multiple murders committed at one time being the hard and fast rule for this classification.

Typically, mass murders are perpetrated by one or more individuals, usually males, and in a single location, or, if committed by an organization, in a string of related incidents which can sometimes take place over an extended period of time. Within that last construct, the killing of large numbers of people by government agents, including the execution of civilians by the police, is also regarded as mass murdering.

People often mistakenly think of serial murder and mass murder as interchangeable tags, but they're not, for it isn't only a higher body count and the scope of the crime that distinguishes a mass murderer, but his motivations as well. Motives which rarely, if ever, involve sexually perverse gratification.

Though at the core of his psyche a mass murderer may harbor the same pathology and homicidal tendencies as a serial killer does, there is much more method to his madness. Revenge, profit, fame, political power…these are the prizes individuals and organizations who kill by the number are hoping to obtain.

In America, you need only say the word "Columbine" now, and measure its lasting impact, to know whether mass murderers Eric Harris and Dylan Klebold achieved similar objectives. Fueled by resentment toward their more successful classmates, when these troubled youths finished their vengeful rampage in April 1999, nearly three-dozen people were wounded; thirteen of whom died, including one teacher.

Deadly school shootings like that one, as well as workplace massacres, have become much too common in the years since, but, still, these violent episodes pale in comparison to state sponsored mass murder campaigns, many of which, once completed, have claimed tens of thousands, even millions, of victims.

Classic examples of state-sponsored mass murder are the shooting of unarmed protestors, the carpet bombing of cities, and the well-orchestrated "cleansing" pogroms targeting ethnic minorities—genocide, sadly, occurring with frightening regularity all throughout the history of mankind. Or, at least, ever since the invention of governments and soldiers and policemen.

When we think of genocide, images of Hitler and Mussolini automatically come to mind. But the record books show they're by no means the only offenders.

In fact, so prevalent are the incidences of government-sanctioned mass murder worldwide that, based upon victim numbers alone, the average profile of a mass murderer turns out *not* to be some outcast teenager shooting up his schoolyard, nor a disgruntled employee "going postal" on the job, but rather an adult male, of any ethnic, who's been officially issued a uniform, badge, and a license to kill.

From crusaders brandishing emblems of the cross while hellishly annihilating Moslems in the holy land, to the Kremlin's secret police arresting 15,000,000 "comrades" and sending them to work to death in the gulags, countries and kings have been ordering their uniformed agents to murder the minions since time immemorial.

And, since time immemorial, many uniformed agents have executed such orders with relish.

The following are just a few famous examples.

1. An inveterate academic lackey who finished last in his class at West Point and who manifested profound symptoms of a narcissistic personality disorder throughout his military career, George Armstrong Custer (pictured above) was the U.S. government's key player in a decades-long pogrom to exterminate the indigenous people of America. In his fixation on establishing himself as their "number one Indian killer" Custer slaughtered thousands of men, women and children, claiming to have killed 200 alone in the battle at Washita *and 900 of their ponies.* By the time the plains Indians staged their famously victorious uprising against him at Little Bighorn, Custer was held in such low regard by them for these atrocities that, reportedly, when they discovered his corpse on the battlefield, no warrior bothered to scalp it because he was considered "too filthy." Today, despite that stunning upset in the war of genocide against them, national census figures reveal that less than 1.5 percent of the U.S. population is Native American, the majority of whom are reduced to living in squalor on designated wastelands.

2. In an obsessive-compulsive bid to rule the entire globe, homicidal drug addict Adolf Hitler used his police and soldiers to kill tens of millions of citizens in little more than a decade. All to lay claim and control over just one small portion called Europe. An indiscriminate hater, Hitler killed everyone and anyone he perceived stood in the way of achieving world dominion, *including his very own generals.* At that rate of mass death, had he gotten his wish and never been stopped, eventually there would've been no one left on the planet for him to lord over.

3. In a highly-organized reign of terror perpetrated for over a century beyond America's successful war against slavery, southern sheriffs and their sworn deputies systematically intimidated, tortured and murdered millions of African Americans, as well as a number of white civil rights workers intent on registering them for the vote. To this day, many of the victims' remains have never been located, their families never properly compensated, and only a fraction of the offenders formally charged and prosecuted.

4. Born Saloth Sar, but far better known as Pol Pot, this self-appointed ruler of Cambodia was yet another bona fide dunce, flunking his college exams three years in a row before being forced to return from Paris to his motherland, his wasted scholarship revoked. With an obvious axe to grind thereafter, Pol Pot would later go on to seize control of the same government who had paid for his education, ordering his uniformed thugs of the Khmer Rouge to arrest, torture and murder nearly 25% of his countrymen—particularly those from the intellectual classes who he almost completely eradicated. In the three years Pol Pot strove to be Cambodia's sole master, he managed to kill an astounding one-million of the mere seven-million people who lived there. Doing the quick math then, and applying that timeframe and his bloodthirsty behavior as a predictor, if Pol Pot had not been ousted from office when he was, this demented individual would've succeeded in killing every one of his fellow Cambodians in only another fifteen years.

5. By Amnesty International's estimates, Uganda's former madman Idi Amin, a practicing cannibal with only a fourth-grade education who insisted on being called "His Excellency President for Life, Field Marshal Alhaji Dr. Idi Amin Dada, VC, DSO, MC, Lord of All the Beasts of the Earth and Fishes of the Seas and Conqueror of the British Empire in Africa in General and Uganda in Particular" directed his police force to arrest, torture and murder approximately 500,000 citizens in his seven-year reign. It should also be noted, Amin had originally seized power in a military coup that was prompted by his fears he was going to be arrested for stealing funds from the Ugandan army, of which he was a commanding officer.

6. For a half century, the supplanted white minority government of South Africa used their police force to brutally oppress the black majority, through the torture and murder of millions of these natural citizens, systematically stealing all their lands and wealth while at the same time forcibly imposing on them conditions of abject poverty.

7. Last but not least, in one of the most unique mass murder events of all time which was executed during Argentina's "Dirty War" through a program dubbed *Operation Condor*, roughly 60,000 citizens were abducted by the Argentine Federal Police and illegally held in secret detention centers where they were interrogated and tortured. Eventually, so there wouldn't be any proof of these crimes, the police sedated their prisoners and then airlifted them out over the middle of the Atlantic Ocean, where they were thrown in alive and drowned.

The badly injured body of 20-year-old Columbia College student Jay Polhill was recovered from Chicago's Little Calumet River today, naked from the waist down. "He didn't have his camera. He didn't have his laptop. He didn't have his wallet…I believe he was murdered." *Polhill's close friend and colleague, commenting on the condition and recovery of the corpse*

"Every night I have to go to sleep thinking about his last moments. It drives me crazy. Was he afraid? Was he hurt? Was he cold?" *Jay Polhill's mother, speaking in 2011 on the anniversary of her son's death*

Chapter 17: Whitewash

CHICAGO, ILLINOIS - MARCH 4, 2010: "A missing Columbia College student was found dead in the Calumet River in South Chicago Tuesday. The partially clad body of Jay Polhill was discovered floating near East 126th Street and South Stony Island Avenue on the far South Side of Chicago. An autopsy was conducted yesterday, but the results were inconclusive.

Twenty-year-old Polhill, a photography major, had last been seen Sunday at his dormitory."

- - -

The beauty of murder, if any, is that there's no Statute of Limitations running on it. So even the perfect kill, once it unravels, as most crime plots invariably do after awhile, can still be investigated and its perps prosecuted at anytime. The case of missing/murdered child Etan Patz is the proof of that; for 33 years gone cold and recently reactivated on brand new evidence.

The only snag in this scheme of justice and the American way is, of course, that you have to get a murder classified as a murder right off the bat, otherwise the case starts to languish within the files of the local police department as an "undetermined" death and, eventually, after six months or so, goes inactive. In the meantime, and as a matter of routine, storefront surveillance videos and cellphone records get wiped clean again, erasing both the victim's and their assailants' trail.

Residents of Chicago Illinois claim this scenario is all the likelier in their city these past few years. They say the Chicago police force has been busy playing a numbers game with crime statistics, trying to feign a decrease in violence on their streets, namely in homicides, and that they've been doing so at the expense of victim families like Jay Polhill's, a young Chicago student and resident who clearly met with some type of foul play in the last days of February 2010.

If this is true, it's really bad news for law abiding citizens, because if the police won't say somebody's been killed when they have been, they won't investigate it either, and then the murderers can breathe and walk free without a fight. And kill again whenever they please to, without fear of being apprehended.

Historically, with its infamous mob families, colorful gangsters and legendary shootouts, Chicago is notorious if not synonymous with crime, so tweaking the numbers today to reflect a sudden downturn or turnaround in criminal activity isn't going to radically change this worldwide perception of the windy city. It's a rep Chicagoans are forever stuck with, like it or not.

In 2011, after the Chicago Police Department released their statistics for the year 2010, reporting in them that violent crime was the lowest it had been *in 45 years*, the CPD was confronted by the press about the possibility its detectives were being pressured to water down serious crime stats.

Clearly vexed by the insinuation, the chief of police curtly replied for the record "absolutely not."

Yet a year after Jay Polhill's undetermined death was upgraded by the medical examiner's office to "drowning due to multiple injuries from assault" the police had still not formally labeled his case a homicide. In fact, Chicago's chief of police informed reporters that it was only recently forwarded to the CPD's cold case division for further analysis.

So is progress just slow then, or is the Polhill murder a perplexing statistical nuisance?

At a glance, the case doesn't seem that complicated: On the evening of February 28th 2010, when Jay Polhill first went missing, he'd told his friends he was going to a party on the opposite side of town.

A third-year photography major at Chicago's Columbia College, he had his camera strapped around his neck and took his laptop with him as well, both items potentially containing important clues as to what may have happened next, but neither of them ever found.

It's likely, in his journeys that night, Polhill may have mistakenly stumbled into a bad neighborhood; Chicago does have a few, I hate to remind. Or perhaps, even more probable, he saw something through his camera lens that he shouldn't have.

There's always stuff going down every night in any major city, and not all of it is good. If it was an event of this nature that the young photographer chanced upon, then maybe, in his artistic opinion, it would have made for an award-winning snapshot, but it's still called being in the wrong place at the wrong time—people engaged in a criminal enterprise, no matter how photogenic, don't usually want their picture taken.

The condition of Polhill's semi-naked body when it was recovered March 2nd 2010 from desolate waters in the Calumet River basin, suggested he was beaten unconscious with a club, a bat, or a similar style of weapon, and thereafter placed into the river where he may have quickly drowned.

An autopsy on the victim revealed multiple blunt force trauma delivered to both sides of the skull and to vertebrae in the neck, while he was still living.

There were some postmortem injuries evidenced on both of his legs too, but these were thought to have been derived from an engine propeller striking his body as it was floating downriver.

Additionally, although the fact his corpse was retrieved nude from the waist down generated some lurid speculation, the Chicago medical examiner did not find any sign of a sexual assault.

Ditto for campus rumors concerning drugs or a drug deal gone sour which were also proven to be unfounded when, weeks later, Polhill's toxicology report showed there were no narcotics or even alcohol in his system at the time that he died.

From the start, Chicago officials had attempted to rule Jay Polhill's death an accidental drowning, even implying a death by suicide, despite the victim having never once displayed or expressed suicidal tendencies. The city's determination finally being overturned wasn't the product of any nagging second thoughts either, but was rather another example of what can be accomplished when a victim's family and friends prod local authorities to consider new evidence, and are willing to part with a pretty penny to hire well-respected outside professionals in order to obtain it.

Behind the scenes, it was a skilled private detective's dedication to Polhill's case and a second forensic pathologist's opinion which led to the city's medical examiner reconsidering her earlier ruling. This was required because, obviously, someone can't take a baseball bat and repeatedly bash their own skull in with it even if they wanted to, so the original decision implying that Polhill did just that, once it was made known to the public, had to be modified to save Chicago's finest from embarrassment.

Now that his death has rightly been reclassified as homicide, at least through the medical examiner's office, the question that must be answered at last is how Polhill ended up in such a remote locale more than twenty miles from his residence, without owning a car, getting a ride from someone, or using his travel pass.

As to bridges or other areas he could have walked across or fallen into the river system from, police insist they reviewed surveillance footage from all of the city's bridges and wharfs and no images of the victim were captured on or near any of them.

It's a modern day murder mystery and the passage of time has certainly deepened it, but the various antemortem fractures and contusions on Polhill's body show this was far from a perfect crime. Hiding it in water may have been meticulously planned, but there were mistakes made in its execution and clearly a lot of things went wrong for the perpetrators, including the possibility that their victim fought back and tried to escape. Simply because two years or more have passed and the identity of the killers still remains a secret does not mean the individuals responsible for this heinous act can't be made to account for it sometime soon.

On the part of law enforcement, this only requires police persistence, a methodical pursuit of the facts to uncover more evidence and eyewitnesses; and a steadfast dedication to enforcing the victim's rights, regardless of who the criminals should turn out to be.

To those ends, the family of Jay Polhill is offering a reward as an incentive for the public's assistance in cracking this case. Visit www.jaypolhill.com for more information.

As mentioned, and at the behest of Polhill's parents, his disappearance and death has finally been reexamined by the Chicago Police Department and it was recently assigned to their Cold Case division for a more active investigation.

Anyone with any information about this matter may now phone 312-746-9690 to speak with a detective, or leave a crime tip on the department's cold case website at http://www.chicagopolice.org/coldcase.

"The Boston College community is deeply saddened by the tragic news out of Saratoga Springs, NY, regarding our missing student. Alexander Grant was an economics major, a member of the College of Arts and Sciences Honors Program, and a gifted and popular student in his class." *Boston College spokesman Jack Dunn commenting in March 2011 on the news of a BC sophomore's disappearance from a Skidmore College house-party in upstate New York and his subsequent drowning.*

"We are deeply saddened by the death of Alexander Grant. The untimely passing of a student is a tragic event in the life of any college; this is a grievous loss for two campus communities. Our hearts go out to Mr. Grant's family and friends. We thank the Saratoga Springs police and all who assisted in the search." *Susan Kress, Acting President of Skidmore College where the victim had been visiting*

"Not only was he my son, but he was my brother and my best friend. Our hearts are broken and we don't particularly want them to heal, but we will carry him with us always." *Kenneth Grant, father of the deceased*

Chapter 18. A Brother, Friend, and Son

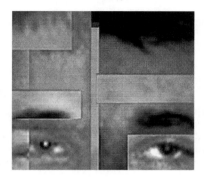

SARATOGA SPRINGS, NEW YORK - MARCH 8, 2011: "Police and rescue personnel announced this morning that they have found the body of Alexander Grant. The 19-year-old was reported missing from a Skidmore house party on Sunday afternoon. His body was discovered entangled in underbrush in the Putnam Creek which is about four-feet-deep and located approximately a quarter mile from where he was last seen on video. Police say Grant's parents and other family members are currently in Saratoga searching for him and have been notified."

- - -

Relatives of the late Alexander Grant do not contest the police and medical examiners' ruling that he died by accident in early March of 2011, nor does it appear they are investigating the matter privately. An overview of his baffling case is being included here only because, in view of video surveillance filmed in the hours allegedly preceding the 19-year-old's drowning and the final police report, his disappearance and death seems more than a little suspicious.

On Saturday, March 5th 2011, Alexander Grant was visiting friends at Skidmore College in upstate New York. According to reports, he arrived at that campus around 8:30 in the evening and two hours later departed with his group to attend a couple of student house parties being held for Spring Break in the nearby resort village of Saratoga Springs. The parties were separate events but on the same street, so Grant and his friends had taken a campus bus downtown to walk to them. They arrived on foot to the first party at approximately 10:30 PM and left for the second one, hosted by Skidmore lacrosse players, very soon thereafter.

According to the Saratoga Springs Police Department, at approximately 11:50 that same night they received a number of noise complaints concerning both house parties and arrived to break up the festivities at half past midnight. The responding officers stated they "had a difficult time controlling the unruly crowd and dispersing the partiers" but did not elaborate beyond this or disclose what means they'd resorted to for scattering them. Police also said they made no arrests and that, once disbanded, the revelers then spilled out onto the streets and headed downtown or back to their campus.

The next day (Sunday), in the early morning hours of March 6th of 2011, an employee at a medical office near the downtown section called the SSPD to report a possible break-in at the facility. When police arrived to check it out, they noted only a small broken window with a considerable amount of blood close by it and bloodstains in the lobby. Other than this, it appeared nothing had been stolen.

In reviewing the video surveillance tape, they reported that a young man, wearing only a long-sleeve tee shirt, boxer shorts and one sock, had entered the premises through the small window at about 1:15 in the morning and stayed in the lobby area for another hour or so. The intruder was also observed to be bleeding at the ankle and "acting disoriented," walking into the walls, stumbling, and falling down.

Later that very same day, at around five in the evening of March 6th, Alexander Grant's friends at Skidmore College also called the Saratoga Springs police, concerned because their guest had not returned to the dorm from the night before and that he hadn't answered any of the texts and voice-messages they'd been leaving for him, either.

According to police reports, Grant's friends informed the SSPD that he had gotten separated from the group at the last party they'd attended and estimated it may have been as early as 11:30 PM since the last time anyone remembered seeing him. The police said they then quickly made a connection between the earlier break-in and the missing young man and immediately organized an all out, high tech search for Grant in the woods surrounding the medical office building as well as along the nearby railroad tracks, only calling off that effort just before midnight because of a major developing snowstorm.

The massive search for Alexander Grant then resumed once more on Monday March 7th, beginning in the morning and lasting until sunset when over a foot of newly fallen snow once again drove the rescuers back.

Tuesday, March 8th, they were out searching again and by noon had at last located the young man's body submerged in a shallow creek a little over a mile from the house party the SSPD had raided.

An autopsy performed in Albany, New York at Albany Medical Center determined Grant had died of asphyxia and hypothermia. The toxicology report would take about another month to deliver, the county medical examiner said, and would hopefully shed more light on the reasons, if any, for the strange events that led to the young man's drowning.

Grant's cellphone was never recovered.

While they waited on the toxicology report, Saratoga Springs police say they began investigating the circumstances that led to Alexander Grant's death and attempted to learn the victim's whereabouts during the hours he could not be accounted for.

That investigation was stymied, the police claim, by the refusal of partygoers and other witnesses to talk to them. They said everyone involved, from Grant's group of friends to the party planners themselves, had immediately hired attorneys and refused to answer even written requests from the SSPD investigators. About this annoying impasse, the Chief of Police publicly declared, "I can tell you we're not getting a lot of cooperation."

Even Grant's family, who had been holding up in this tragedy remarkably well, and were only seeking answers not retribution, expressed their frustration with the wall of silence. They sent an open letter to the press stating they were, "distraught at the unfortunate span of critical hours that lapsed" and "we don't believe we've been told everything we need to know about this by Alex's friends."

By April, in hopes of ending this standoff, immunity from prosecution for any and all minor offenses that might be related to the case was actually being offered by the authorities in exchange for information about the night Grant had gone missing.

And still, out of fear of the police, or loathing, nobody was willing to come forward.

To make matters worse, results from the postmortem toxicology test were also not forthcoming, and, as the stalemate continued well into August of 2011, there was still no official word on whether Alexander Grant had had any drugs and alcohol in his system that might serve to explain his bizarre behavior captured on tape the night of March 5th.

A spokesman for the SSPD, when quizzed about this unusual delay said he could furnish, "no answers as to why it might be" and another county official implied that there'd been a "surprising" *lack* of results in the test, such that it was possible Grant's sample had been resubmitted to another lab for a more extensive battery of tests.

Finally, on September 21st 2011, Saratoga County officials ended the suspense, announcing that Grant's second and final toxicology report revealed no drugs or narcotics had contributed to his death. The meager 0.11 blood/alcohol content "raises more questions than answers," the District Attorney conceded, adding that, "we still don't know what affected his body to such a significant degree, which then led to the circumstances that caused his death."

Grant's parents too, although hugely relieved that drugs were not responsible for their son's demise, agreed that it still left them in the dark about "how the young man we loved so much could have sustained the state of disorientation that characterized his last few hours on this earth."

The SSPD's release to the public of their investigative summary nine days later on September 30th 2011 would add yet two more puzzling pieces to an already boggling picture of the Grant disappearance and drowning.

In this press release, possibly the longest of its kind in history, the Saratoga Springs police inexplicably upped the victim's BAC finding from the 0.11 level previously reported by Albany County to 0.16 instead. They also newly referenced video surveillance they say they uncovered which showed Grant wandering around the downtown train depot in a state of confusion at 11:30 PM, the night he first went missing.

However, they do not explain why this important documentation wasn't offered sooner or why it was never before mentioned. Nor why Grant would have left a party without his friends which he'd only been at for less than a half hour.

"The case will remain open," the Saratoga Springs police stated, "in the hope that someone or some item of evidence will provide the critical information needed to complete the investigation." The SSPD's entire press brief on the Grant incident reads as follows:

"Saratoga Springs Police have finished examining the active leads in the investigation into the death of Alexander Grant during the early morning hours of March 6, 2011. A summary of the investigation is below. Much of the information contained herein has been released on prior occasions.

"On March 5, 2011 Alexander Grant, 19-years-of-age from Briarcliff Manor, NY who is a student at Boston College, travels to Saratoga Springs during his spring break to meet with friends who are attending Skidmore College. He arrives in Saratoga Springs sometime before 8:30 PM, picks up a friend in the downtown area

and travels to Skidmore College. He plans to stay with a friend in one of the dorms on campus.

"Between his arrival in Saratoga Springs and 10:28 PM when he boards a bus on the Skidmore Campus, Grant and several others are drinking beer and tequila in one of the dorm rooms. At 10:28 PM, Grant and the group of people he is with board a bus at Skidmore and then is dropped off at the intersection of Clinton and Van Dam Streets.

"They then walk to a party at 146 Church Street where Grant is reported to be last seen dancing with a female between 11:00 and 11:30 PM. Two female Skidmore students are identified as having contact with Grant at the party however both report that Grant was only there for a short time before he went to another part of the house and they never saw him again. Grant's friend loses track of him at the party and assumes that Grant has met up with someone else and that they would re-connect at a later time. His friend sends approximately 6 text messages to Grant between 11:37 PM and noon on March 6 asking where he is and giving Grant the address of the dorm room. All of the people who report seeing Grant at the party state that they left the party when the police arrived to break it up at about 12:30 AM.

"Surveillance video at the train station on Station Lane off of West Avenue in Saratoga Springs shows Alexander Grant walking to the front of the building from Station Lane at 11:31 PM. He is alone, fully clothed and appears to be staggering as he walks. Grant is observed walking around the building to the train tracks behind and then is last seen heading north along the tracks towards the Church Street overpass. No other people or vehicles are observed coming or going from the train station. He is last seen at the train station at 11:34 PM.

"At 1:33 AM surveillance video at 3 Care Lane captures Alexander Grant kicking in a small 3×3 window at the entrance to the building. He squeezes inside and is now observed to be wearing only one sock, a long sleeve white shirt and shorts. He appears to have already fallen outside, as there is dirt on his back upon his entry to the building. Grant has cut himself and is bleeding considerably. He never leaves the lobby area or attempts to break into any of the offices. He appears disoriented and/or intoxicated. He is stumbling into the walls and repeatedly loses his balance. He eventually staggers out of the building once again at 2:11 AM and is last seen walking away from the building. Any blood trail that may have been left by Grant at that time was washed away by heavy rains during the day on the 6th, prior to police being notified of the break-in at 12:36 PM.

"Police are notified of the break-in at 12:36 PM on the 6th. A brief search of the area for evidence related to the burglary is conducted as police have no missing person report until 4:47 PM when Grant's friend and another student arrive at Police Headquarters and report that Grant has not been seen since the party on Church Street. No additional evidence of the burglary is located during the initial search.

"Grant is quickly identified as the person observed on the Care Lane surveillance video and an intensive search of the area is immediately begun. An approaching severe winter storm reduces the amount of time police and fire personnel will be able to search on the night of the 6th. New York State Forest Rangers are unable to respond during the night due to the storm and New York State Police Aviation is unable support the effort that night. Thermal imaging units were employed without success. The Saratoga County Reverse 911 system was activated, reaching 7,000 landlines within a half-mile radius of Care Lane generating any leads or reported sightings.

"Small search teams begin searching the area to the north and west of the Care Lane area, along the railroad tracks, and including the buildings at Sunnyside Gardens. One search team located Grant's pants and wallet on top of a snow bank between the Care Lane building and the railroad tracks. Another search team located footprints in the snow along the railroad tracks. There was only one set of footprints that traveled north along the tracks occasionally entering the woods, circling dense brush and then returning to the tracks. One set of tracks leading into the woods towards Putnam Creek was observed and a visual check of the creek was made without success. The tracks were lost and no other tracks were observed further north. By this time the storm had become too severe for further searching and all search teams were called back to the command post.

"On the morning of March 7th, an intensive search with additional manpower was begun at about 10:30 AM with improving weather conditions. Searching continued all day on the 7th until dark. Search teams again were sent out on March 8th at 9:45 AM and at 10:43 AM, Saratoga Springs Fire Department personnel located Alexander Grant's body submerged in Putnam Creek under an ice shelf in about four feet of water approximately 30 yards from where the last set of foot prints were seen during the search on the night of the 6th.

"Chief of Police Christopher Cole and Public Safety Commissioner Richard Wirth made notification of the recovery of Alexander Grant's body to his parents.

"The body was turned over to Coroner John Demartino and Dr. Michael Sikiricka at Albany Medical Center performed an autopsy on March 9.

"The cause of death is officially listed as asphyxia due to drowning with contributing factors of intoxication and probable hypothermia. At the time of his death Alexander Grant had a blood alcohol content of 0.16%. A low level of THC (marijuana) was also detected. Injuries sustained by Mr. Grant were consistent with someone who had been stumbling through the woods with no indication of injuries consistent with an assault observed. As noted by Saratoga County District Attorney James Murphy previously, two toxicology tests were run with several hundred drugs being screened for. Other than the alcohol and marijuana, no other drugs were detected in Grant's system at the time of his death. The known facts of the case tend to support the conclusion made regarding the cause of death. Alexander Grant apparently became lost and disoriented due to his level of intoxication and suffering from the effects of hypothermia tragically fell into Putnam creek and was unable to pull himself to safety.

"Police do not suspect foul play in the death of Alexander Grant. However, police have tried unsuccessfully to interview the occupants of the 146 Church Street apartment. With the exception of one of the occupants, who police spoke with last week, all have decline written requests by police to their attorneys to make them available for interviews. The friend that Alexander Grant had come to visit and planned to stay with while in Saratoga Springs has also decided not to speak with police any further and has obtained legal counsel.

"Police have stressed that the priority of this investigation is to determine what happened to Alexander Grant. Saratoga County District Attorney James Murphy has offered immunity from prosecution for anyone who may have information relating to what happened to Alexander Grant but fears being arrested for minor disorderly conduct or alcohol related charges.

"Police have located the source of the alcohol for the Church Street party, which was legally purchased by someone over 21 years of age. Police were first notified of the party on Church Street at about 11:50 PM, nearly 20 minutes after Alexander Grant is captured on surveillance video at the train station. Patrol units were eventually able to respond, and arrived at 12:25 AM on the 6th. Police had a difficult time controlling the unruly crowd and dispersing the partiers. While doing so they were unable to build enough probable cause to arrest anyone for furnishing alcohol to minors at the party. None of the occupants at the time of the party currently reside there.

"As for the drinking that occurred in the dorm room at Skidmore College. None of the participants was of age. Police do not know how the alcohol was obtained, but do know that alcohol was consumed in the room, including by Alexander Grant. Again, the source of the alcohol at the dorm room was a secondary consideration during the early phases of the investigation. By the time police were able to focus on this aspect of the case, potential witnesses were uncooperative and police were not able to locate independent evidence of the source of the alcohol in the dorm room. In consultation with Saratoga County District Attorney James Murphy and in consideration of court decisions and the facts of the case, a decision has been made not to charge any of the occupants of the room with a criminal offense.

"Police do not know how or why Alexander Grant came to be at the train station at 11:31 PM. Based on the time of the video, Grant was at the party on Church Street for considerably less than one hour. He appears in the video, walking alone and apparently intoxicated. Police have been unable to locate anyone who saw or had contact with Grant between the time he left the party and the time he appears at the train station. Several phone messages and text messages were sent to his cell phone between 11:37 PM and noon of the following day, however Grant never answered and his cell phone was never recovered. It is important to note that no one and no vehicles approach the train station for a considerable amount of time before or after Grant appears on the video.

"By the time Alexander Grant appears at the Care Lane location, he has not only shed some of his clothing but he appears quite disoriented, probably suffering from the effects of hypothermia. In addition, on March 9th an employee of 7 Care Lane found Alexander Grant's Boston College ID in the snow next to the door. The door to 7 Care Lane has a swipe card lock system similar to the system at the entrances to the buildings at Boston College. Along with the footprints in the snow that enter the woods and circle dense brush repeatedly, this indicates that Alexander Grant was considerably disoriented.

"At this point the Saratoga Springs Police have no more active leads. However the case will remain open in the event that someone comes forward with information about the critical time period between when Grant leaves the party and he arrives at the train station. Grant's shoes and cell phone were never recovered and if found may give police additional information on his route of travel and therefore additional possible leads. Police will leave the investigation open in the hope that someone or some item of evidence will provide the critical information needed to complete the investigation.

"The family of Alexander Grant will continue to be advised of any developments in the case. Once again, the Saratoga Springs Police offer their condolences, and their support to the Grant family."

At present, over one year later, the Grant case still remains open as was promised, but it is not being actively investigated and no one who witnessed Grant's final hours have furnished any testimonies.

In the time since his passing, because the young man was involved in so many philanthropic activities in his short life, his family created a scholarship memorial in his name. The Alexander Maxwell Grant Foundation provides funding to disadvantaged students studying the visual and music arts. Visit www.AlexGrant.org for more information about Alexander Grant and this charitable organization.

"When I looked at these cases, the first thing that jumped out at me was the victimological profile. It's not a normal distribution…the standard deviation is only 0.4 on their weight and height." *Dr. Lee Gilbertson, gang specialist and associate professor, Department of Criminal Justice Studies at St. Cloud University*

"The statistics are so stacked against this number of men, young men, Caucasian males, found in bodies of water in that cluster of states, within that period of time." *Dr. Cyril Wecht, forensic pathologist*

"The probability is virtually zero that five intoxicated students just happened to walk similar or even different routes and end up on the riverbank." *Dr. Maurice Godwin, criminal investigative psychologist, commenting on the La Crosse Wisconsin drowning cluster*

"They could have been murdered but the person was just so good at doing it that they didn't leave any physical evidence…[they] could sedate and drown him in a tub or something like that and then throw him in the river." *John Kelly, psychotherapist and profiler*

Chapter 19: Probable Causes and Statistics
Serial Drownings, Serial Murders, or Other?

Thanks to private investigators and a vigilant public, there has been more attention paid to the disappearances of young men in the I-90 and I-94 corridor in recent years. While this hasn't put an end to the fifteen-year phenomena of drowning deaths, spotlighting the issue is definitely progress of some kind, even if a consensus about it hasn't been reached yet. Even if it's discourse presently dominating the discussion, and official attempts at silencing it.

Many working theories have sprung from this interest, many more are still in formation, but only one of these will eventually solve the drowning riddle and, hopefully, when acted upon, stop the dying. Only one can restore our rivers and lakes to the playgrounds they once were, instead of the killing fields they've become since 1997.

The ruling theory will be that which, after a thorough debate, answers every question in the conundrum and holds up to a rigorous statistical inquiry. Measuring any theory against statistical probabilities is the prime method for determining its integrity. Within this will be a margin of error, quite small generally, which takes into account the influence of chance and coincidence, and other extraordinarily rare occurrences.

From most popular to fringe, this chapter will examine and rate the prominent theories of the day concerning the drowning men syndrome in the northland. While it won't be possible to analyze every single one currently in existence or in creation, all of them will be sorted and encompassed to some degree in two distinct categories: *Serial Drownings* and *Serial Murders*, and then this section will conclude with *Other* less considered possibilities that the overall statistics might logically lead to.

We begin with the official explanation: accidental drownings.

SERIAL DROWNINGS: This is the prevailing theory offered every time by law enforcement officials, and the only one widely supported by crime agencies and committees such as the FBI and the Center for Homicide Research. That being the case, it's gotten plenty of airtime already and I won't belabor a description and analysis of it here. In short, the serial drowning theory is a blood simple explanation—people are becoming profoundly intoxicated and somehow ending up in nearby bodies of water and drowning. However, as has already been demonstrated, this theory isn't statistically supportable and neither is it backed up by all the evidence, the primary reason why the idea of serial drowning is constantly being challenged.

Plain and simple, America has a diverse population and we have no laws preventing anyone from freely socializing in public or in private. Thus, "people" drinking in U.S. clubs, bars, and taverns equals men *and* women, young *and* old, popular *and* unpopular, academically successful *and* scholastically inept, athletic *and* out of shape, light-skinned *and* persons of color, tall *and* short, thin *and* overweight, etc.

Additionally, Americans have become very mobile, almost nomadic if you will, in the past few decades. Regularly relocating for employment or training opportunities has become routine for us. That means, regardless of region or climate, this diverse population mix now exists everywhere and anywhere one goes in the United States, college towns included. For police to adamantly state, year after year, that a clear and definable victimology doesn't exist along the Corridor of Death is therefore quite a stretch. And for them to also adamantly insist that alcohol is the real killer, when most of the victims' BAC test levels show they weren't profoundly drunk or on any other mind-altering substance when they died, is equally farfetched.

Thus this, the most popular theory of them all, is on its face the least statistically probable of any being offered to date, except, perhaps, for "alien abductions" and (my favorite) "alien medical experiments" gone awry.

But can the authorities really be wrong about this if so many are in agreement? Yes, it has happened all throughout history. Remember that once upon a time the authorities insisted the world was flat, and anybody who disagreed with them was sent to prison. Or executed.

SERIAL MURDERS: This section will address the main idea of a serial killer, but will also have to be broken down into subsets thereof because, while the Smiley Face theory is the most publicized explanation at the moment, it is not the only serial murder theory out there. It may as well be a misnomer for investigator Gannon's original precept, as he never once said that a smiley face signature was the absolute linkage in the drowning mystery.

A Serial Murderer: The statistics do readily support the basic concept of a serial murderer roaming the northern corridor. A serial murderer utilizing highways to reach a specific type of prey is not completely unheard of, particularly if his profession requires him to travel on a regular basis.

Having said that, the territory is much too large for one alone to negotiate, not only in its breadth, but because as many as three abductions are simultaneously occurring within only a matter of hours or days, and these are happening in locations at least a hundred miles or more from each other. No one, not even the omnipotent Dr. Hannibal Lecter, can be in two places at one time, never mind three.

Moreover, while a solitary serial killer is, statistically speaking, the most typical type of such predators, the experts are correct in asserting that these are psychotically compelled individuals and usually have a very clear motif and predictable behavior pattern as a result of that psychosis, from which none so far have ever truly varied.

Stalking, abducting, torturing, sexually assaulting, mutilating and, finally, murdering a victim, is the name of their sick game, without exception. I have studied well over 100 of these drowning cases in some detail and there is just not strong enough evidence on the recovered corpses of torture, mutilation, and sexual assault presenting in the majority of them. No major wounds and missing limbs or appendages, a vital theme of serial murdering, is therefore noticeably absent.

Granted, dead men tell no tales and those found floating in water tend to be the least talkative, but your classic serial killer is not typically satisfied with a fast kill, either—drowning someone only takes minutes, so that manner of death, for a serial murderer, isn't going to be quite as titillating as has been suggested by some theorists.

Nor do such killers get pleasure from a kill that leaves very few if any marks on a victim. When most of the drown victims display no signs whatsoever of physical trauma, either antemortem or postmortem, then that is the clear motif itself which has to be properly paired to a prospective murderer, which in this case just isn't going to come under the average serial murderer profile, or none known to date.

I feel this point is also underscored by the fact that the alleged serial killer's signature/s, when (and if) drawn at a body-dumping scene, is never identical with any other one alleged to have been previously left by him. Sometimes, in fact, no graffiti is left behind at all.

A signature is a signature and, discounting the issue of forgeries which isn't relevant here, will always reveal its true author, time and time again, despite not knowing what his actual name may be, or the arrival of a copycat. Also, though not all serial killers do leave the police or the press messages at their murder scenes, when one chooses to, he doesn't stop doing it or leave them intermittently. Instead, it becomes an inextricable part of his crime pattern, this public form of bragging.

Based on that analysis, I don't believe a serial murderer, even the most "organized" type, has the kind of self-control and mobility to commit these kind of killings. The logistics and statistics don't support it.

A Serial Murdering Gang: The idea of a group of people executing murders in a large region isn't implausible, depending on who this alleged group is supposed to be and what their motives are. A gang, in its traditional sense, however, is most unlikely. Gang crime is territorial in nature, doesn't often extend beyond certain limited boundaries, and gang murder is resorted to as an extreme method of enforcement and/or revenge, not just for sport or pleasure. It's feasible a hit may be ordered against someone in another location beyond a gang's known borders (former members and/or snitches usually the targets) but these murders would be few and far between, and the victim known by and familiar with his assailants.

As well, gangs of this origin almost exclusively arise out of economic deprivation and these conditions of impoverishment remain largely unimproved for most gang members regardless of their lifelong membership. To drive several hundreds of miles on the interstate regularly would require a reliable and inconspicuous mode of transportation, and poverty typically precludes the luxury of automobile ownership. Of course, as with any organization, criminal or legit, there is a hierarchy in place in a gang too, but the wealth and status of those few on the upper tier is fairly transient due to the frequency of arrests and incarcerations or assassinations from rivals. So the idea of gangs, as we know them now, to equip themselves expressly so they can travel weekly or monthly well outside the central hub of their turf and activities, for any reason, is further rendered specious.

And it also bears repeating, no ordinary serial murderers do their "work" in teams.

Internet Killers: Within the same theory of gang-organized slayings, an internet gang of gamer types who network online to kill for sport has also been recently introduced. There are different schemes offered as to the mechanics of such a groups' leadership and their possible motivations, some not too credible, but overall I think this is an excellent example of the sort of critical thinking that experts have been recommending be put to use.

We've all seen how the internet has bred a certain criminality of its own and the ability for anonymous individuals and groups to commit large scale crimes against a huge number of people, in most cases without their ever knowing it.

But that's just the point. Those crimes are taking place *solely* via the Internet, facilitated and executed entirely through cyberspace, and the perps are mainly motivated by greed, or, in the case of hackers, political beliefs and agendas. More often than not, the co-conspirators of cybercrime have never even met before in the physical world, and don't even know each others' real legal names. Just handles and aliases and e-mail addresses.

There have been isolated instances where some with serious criminal intent have sought to prearrange fatal face-to-face meetings with their victims in online chatrooms or on social media sites, and then sealed the deal through direct messaging once they won that person's trust. These travesties, however, aren't as common as you read about. They only get top billing in the news because it's a subject that hits home for many of us. We all to some extent use the internet now to communicate with the world and to socialize with people we have only ever virtually "met". It's scary too because many of us interact in this way on the very websites where someone else less lucky "hooked up" with the wrong site member.

But, again, these aren't necessarily group acts or even highly-orchestrated ones. And they couldn't account for hundreds of deaths of a certain type of victim by a select group in a specific region over a protracted period of time, because, thankfully, it takes just one or two such criminal misdeeds before these sloppy felons manage to get arrested.

An online gamer is a new and unique creature, of course, and anyone so preoccupied with violence and with earning scores and prestige by exhibiting superior skills at being *virtually* violent, will understandably draw suspicion from onlookers. Especially when people are earnestly trying to explain otherwise senseless killings. I'm not dismissing it as preposterous, but in rating its plausibility one also has to consider that a devout gamer *plays* games and has very little interest in the "real world" with just as little real world contact. They are then the quintessential introvert, saddled with the same heightened fears as introverts have always had and found so socially debilitating. Picturing this personality profile gearing up to cruise a bar for a victim or rendezvousing with others in a group to do the same is difficult at best.

Also, if elite gamers could indeed conquer agoraphobia long enough to become real-time hunters and slayers, they'd certainly want their scores and ranks to be posted someplace on the web so everyone could envy and admire their achievements and prowess. Not to mention that somebody someday would flub up and boast elsewhere to the wrong person about their new hobby, and inadvertently give the whole weird operation away. Erring in this manner much sooner than fifteen years.

All of the above observations, in essence, revealing a pretty bad rap against the gaming community for their unabashedly antisocial predilections, but a murder theory that has no legs when it comes to practical application.

Cult Killers: Ritualistic killings by a coven of Satanists comes close on the heels of gamers in terms of probability and statistics. For one, I have never met a bona fide devil worshipper and I bet you haven't either. In fact, I'm inclined to regard such practitioners—judging by the dearth of them—as more a product of Hollywood and certain paranoid religious faiths than a realistic threat to society and/or its virgins. Still, even if deviating from what they're trying to emulate, what a group subscribes to and what they believe they are about will dictate their clandestine activities. Sacrificing young men for the glory of Satan can't be ruled out entirely as a motive then…except for the problem that there aren't signs of ritual evidenced on any of the victims.

Clergy Killings: On this same theme of religious extremism, but for different reasons, I don't give much credence to a group of serial murdering priests or monks, either. Cloistered clergyman are, I suspect, feared and despised today much more for the pedophiles among them and to whom they have frequently given safe harbor than for any secret, diabolical plots to serial kill. Pedophiles are a major menace in any costume they devise to cloak themselves in, but they're not murderers usually, and the drown victims are grown men not small children. It may be worthy of delving deeper into this from a historical angle, though, since who knows that there isn't some connection from the victims' distant past, but as of today I have seen no mention on any discussion board of this remote possibility.

Numerical Equations: I have seen and tried to follow threads by people admirably attempting to draw parallels between names and numbers and locations to see if there is a maniacal math being employed by the killer or killers. Cryptograms, anagrams, numerical puzzles…this is a fascinating line of thought and sometimes I myself think, if only for a fleeting moment, that I can also detect the pattern being deciphered by the poster, or other ones on my own. But each time it only proves to be another dead end when formula after formula fails to neatly link up all the victims to each other.

Numbers are intrinsically important in this matter, I agree, and we can easily count in excess of 200 drown victims by now, an unprecedented tally for any serial slayer. But if there really is one particular person, or a gang, killing at such a high rate for so long, then this has to happen before we can find them: Somehow all those drowning cases must link together.

OTHER: The idea of rogue cops, off duty cops, retired cops, or cop impersonators killing young men and dumping their bodies in water has also been bandied about in many discussion forums. In fact, it's one of the oldest theories within the Smiley Face Murder theory and is still going strong in popularity. This might also account for law enforcement's hostility to the I-90 and I-94 serial killer concept and their relentless efforts to debunk it, as blatant inferences to police corruption and brutality aren't likely to win their hearts and minds over. It also complicates their job of maintaining law and order if the public inherently doesn't trust them.

Cops killing the serial killer theory, therefore, has become a necessity, and job one in those areas dense with suspicious fatalities.

But, regardless of the power of those who may oppose it, a good conspiracy theory never dies because it always ably answers two important things: why a governing authority desires to quash it, and the unexplained.

I've already intimated that I don't believe there are any serial murderers at work in the northern corridor, and I also think that the graffiti, if genuine, is so all over the board with borrowed "signatures" from past serial killers who've been apprehended as to suggest it's being planted by parties with a criminal justice education, and who are calculatingly using these symbols and phrases as a clever diversion.

Discounting serial murder seemed an obvious conclusion to reach when fully reviewing the matter, not only because of the enormous size of the area the drownings are occurring in, or for the want of a clear and classic killer motif in these deaths, but because there's just too many of them. Serial killers, operating individually or sometimes in duos, may kill a dozen people or so, perhaps two or three dozen over the same length of time we're talking about here—body counts which are nothing to scoff at or make light of to be sure—but when discussing this volume of killing, hundreds of suspicious deaths, then it falls well within the realm of mass murdering, not serial. And mass murder, as I've demonstrated already, falls under a much different category. A broader one that would tie up the loose ends we're seeing in the drowning men syndrome, and connect the victims without there ever having to be a formal connection between them.

Police don't want to be regarded as suspects, and they truly resent the public's growing distrust of them, but that distrust is not founded on irrational fears. Like men of the Cloth, men in uniform have also abused their authority and the days of blind admiration and respect for them, unfortunately, are long gone. In the age of cellphone cameras, camcorders, and Twitter, it's become much harder for officers to hide excessive use of force, citizen profiling, or outright murders, and all one has to do now is Google the phrase "police corruption" or anything similar to see officer misconduct is rampant even in first-world democracies like our own.

Shooting teargas and rubber bullets at peaceful, unarmed protestors, beating someone restrained in handcuffs, tasering prisoners to the brink of death or beyond, racially profiling African Americans on the roads and on the sidewalks, raping female motorists in routine traffic stops…reports and images of these alarming violations are all over the web and can no longer be covered up or explained away.

In the 21st century, in America's "war against terrorism" which seems to have no end, police powers have expanded exponentially while citizens' rights have been drastically diminished. And still there is no real oversight committee policing the police for reports of being heavy-handed. The police themselves review such complaints through their Internal Affairs divisions and rarely side with a petitioner.

Amnesty International has sent up red flags about the enhanced powers and new technology of police forces around the world. They have also issued repeated warnings of late about the widespread misuse by officers of taser guns which cause neuromuscular paralysis, leave very few marks on the body, and can be employed to brutalize and torture citizens without fear these crimes will be discovered. A country of particular concern to them is the United States where this so called nonlethal weapon has been available since the 1970's when it was first invented and distributed.

Ever since the late 1990's, the deployment of taser guns to police departments has swollen to now include practically every state in the union. Organizations like Amnesty International say many hundreds of U.S. deaths in the past decade or more are attributable to police officers repeatedly tasering subjects during and after arrests, the deadly side effects of which are amplified for victims who have alcohol in their systems or narcotics.

Amnesty even released data that shows the majority of those tasered by police were in fact unarmed and committing either minor or no offenses at all which would have merited the use of any type of physical force against them.

Similarly, human rights groups are also ringing alarm bells about a rising number of deaths of U.S. citizens in police custody. They say the creation and use of a new classification by police and medical examiners to justify these deaths as caused by "Excited Delirium" is a very worrisome trend. It should also be noted, this dubious diagnosis has no basis in medicine and is not recognized by any medical board or institution.

Undoubtedly one of the worse examples on record of police abuse in the United States, and the dismal failure of Internal Affairs to investigate it and prosecute the offenders, happened in recent times and was exposed through the infamous Rampart Scandal of the Los Angeles Police Department during the 1990's.

The Rampart Scandal refers to the criminally corrupt police assigned to the *Community Resources Against Street Hoodlums* (CRASH) anti-gang unit of the LAPD's Rampart Division. When it finally imploded, more than 70 officers with ties to the CRASH crime-ring were implicated for perpetrating major criminal offenses against their community, making it one of the largest documented cases of police misconduct in the history of the United States.

The crimes of the CRASH police unit were highly-organized and executed, and included unprovoked shootings, murders and beatings; planting of false evidence; witness intimidation; framing of innocent citizens; evidence tampering and destruction; murder-for-hire schemes; gun-for-hire schemes; stealing and dealing narcotics; bank robbery; perjury; and conspiring to cover up proof of these illegal acts.

Sanctioned by certain higher-ups in the Los Angeles Police Department who had knowledge of the unit's existence and mission, most if not all of the CRASH officers involved in the scandal were found to have advanced their careers and financially profited in other ways from their numerous criminal activities.

A deep probe from outside investigative agencies into the clandestine culture of the elite CRASH police unit also disclosed another chilling find: CRASH member officers had a special logo tattooed on their bodies, a skull wearing a cowboy hat encircled with poker cards depicting the "dead man's hand" of eights and aces.

The special gang-buster cops had become, in every possible way, a gang unto themselves.

In the case of the drowning men, people don't have to go on an elaborate fishing expedition to find questionable links to their own law enforcement officials: Before, during and after, police are somehow always involved in young men's disappearances, and they never seem to be handling themselves or the subsequent death investigations properly.

Public scrutiny and speculation may frustrate police departments and make even the most honest cop feel they're trapped in a damned-if-you-do and damned-if-you-don't position, but sweeping curious deaths under a rug and/or maligning victims' reputations, if that's all they're guilty of, only adds to doubt about their role in the drownings.

And is that doubt so unwarranted when the public is in pursuit of what they believe to be a network of secretive killers with an ability to overtake and disable a full grown man and enough knowledge of forensics and police procedure to disguise a murder as a drowning?

I don't think so. As a matter of fact, I rate this popular version of the Smiley Face Murder theory to be the most statistically probable of any I have come across yet. Because, as Southern police forces have already shown us back in the 20th century, it wouldn't require an actual conspiracy per se to pull off something of this magnitude. It requires only a dangerous belief of being above the law, a deplorable habit of overstepping authority, and a cover-for-your-brother mentality to be triggered in any investigating officers who didn't participate in the homicides themselves, but who suspected police culpability upon a closer review and hoped to protect their colleagues.

How does it work then, if not through a conspiracy of killer cops killing intentionally? Perhaps at its most malevolent it may be akin to "Firefighter's Arson" a not so rare occurrence whereby a fireman finds perverse gratification in starting an inferno and later also gets to play hero by helping to put it out.

So, fire versus water, the cops who may be involved in intentionally "drowning" men for thrills and spills would probably be water recovery experts, or ones with strong ties to related professions.

But maybe a far more logical and benign scenario might resemble this one: A young man leaves a party or bar slightly inebriated. It's late and he's exhausted, maybe even irritated because he had an argument with someone before he left the place. He's walking home, but not in a manner as coordinated as usual. Along the way he might also pause where he shouldn't in order to empty his bladder. Or perhaps he's just wearing his hood up and somehow looks suspicious to cops cruising by. They pull over and get out to interrogate the man, but he's not doing anything wrong he tells them and "pulls an attitude" which the police find annoying and disrespectful. That earns the guy the stun-gun treatment. They shock him once, twice, three times maybe. After which the victim falls to the ground comatose and unresponsive, or dies.

Wrongful death, suspensions without pay, demotions, lawsuits…the river is close by. It's a no brainer what to do.

"A sense of confidence in the courts is essential to maintain the fabric of ordered liberty for a free people and three things could destroy that confidence and do incalculable damage to society: that people come to believe that inefficiency and delay will drain even a just judgment of its value; that people who have long been exploited in the smaller transactions of daily life come to believe that courts cannot vindicate their legal rights from fraud and over-reaching; that people come to believe the law—in the larger sense—cannot fulfill its primary function to protect them and their families in their homes, at their work, and on the public streets."

Chief Justice Warren E. Burger, U.S. Supreme Court

Chapter 20: "You Can't See What You're Not Looking For"

This bold statement, "you can't see what you're not looking for," drawn with a smiley-faced *o* and an eye sketched neatly into the hump of the *n*, was allegedly left by the killer or killers at the scene of one young man's drowning. If it is true that this graffiti message comes directly from a group of serial murderers, then, whoever the miscreants are, they're quite right and we should take them up on their dare.

It's an interesting expression outside of that context too, because, apart from being a potential clue in the case of the drowning men, and disclosing that the author who scrawled it on the wall is fairly literate, (knowing to use "you're" correctly instead of the much-misappropriated "your"), this phrase is also a popular song lyric from a band who contributed music to the even more popular slash horror film series, *Scream*. The first installment of which appeared in theatres in 1996.

The plot to *Scream* and *Scream 2, Scream 3*, etc., is brutally simple and reliably formulaic: There's a ruthless killer of young people on the loose and everybody's either trying not to be the next victim or attempting desperately to catch him.

Where the *Scream* films do break tradition with the genre, however, is that the actual killer himself can be a different person every time. That is to say, anybody who wears the killer mask, which resembles the face in Edvard Munch's classic painting "The

Scream", can do the serial slayings. A repetitive theme to these movies which can go on indefinitely, of course, or until moviegoers decide they've finally gotten bored with the franchise and move on to something else.

Again, I'm not saying that this is the same motif at play in the fifteen-year slew of suspicious drownings in the northern corridor. But I'm also not saying that it isn't.

What I am saying is, if investigators prefer to only look at alcohol as the common link in all these strange deaths, then that is what they can and will find without fail. But to do this they also have to ignore the many cases where autopsy reports and toxicology findings simply don't support such a theory. Not to mention that the victim class doesn't represent an adequate enough cross section of the population for it all to be just a tragic coincidence.

It's shocking that, in most of the cases, the facts aren't even being fully considered. A presumption is immediately made by the police and when the evidence they uncover doesn't conform to that, it's all tossed to the wind. In fact, oftentimes police search-and-rescue efforts aren't even being launched in a timely and professional manner, further hampering an already compromised inquiry.

For example, in one of the newer disappearances I'd been tracking since this winter, I was appalled to see a one-day police search for a missing student abruptly abandoned, solely on the word of an unnamed source claiming they'd heard someone yelling for help down by the river the night the victim went missing.

Of course, from having just objectively looked at it all through a forensic perspective, we now know that drowning people can't speak or yell, for lack of air. So perhaps the young man in question was calling for help from somewhere other than the riverbank. His drowned corpse was found floating three days later by his family and friends in the area where he allegedly disappeared, although, calculating the water temperatures and the equally chilly weather, his body shouldn't have resurfaced for at least two to three more weeks, or longer.

Just another "classic" drowning, the police and medical examiner proclaimed, and, as has become customary for these events, the toxicology report which revealed an unremarkable blood/alcohol content didn't change that verdict. This, even though the victim's BAC level was nowhere near what would have been required for him to head in the wrong direction to his apartment *and* fall into the river on his way.

But at least the 21-year-old birthday boy and honor student was found in the spot where that helpful anonymous "witness" claimed he'd be located.

When attempting to address community concerns over a plaguing situation like this one, public officers are bound by duty and oath to answer 100% truthfully 100% of the time, and to take action where warranted without prejudice. I emphasize this because authorities responding to this matter in the past had to know they were basing their opinions and assurances on statistics that are irrelevant. All of them had to realize the obvious; that, whatever the cause or causes, there is a disproportional representation among the drown victims, and that it's not the element of intoxication that is uniformly connecting their deaths, but the young men themselves. *Who they are and what makes them so outstanding is setting them up as targets.*

Arguing otherwise is no different than saying young, popular, academically successful, athletic males of medium build have suddenly developed a genetic predisposition to walking into icy waters and perishing. Worded in that way, anybody could recognize that such a contention has no merit. And yet this is, in effect, what authorities are always saying.

It's bad science and police-work. A mindset. Observational bias. Groupthink.

On the subject of police work and public safety, it needs to be pointed out again and again that, in spite of security cameras, foot patrols, a stepped up police presence, fences, safe buses, and whatever other measures have been employed to prevent it, these mysterious disappearances ending in death have continued in full force to the present. Indeed, there are so many safeguards in place today that, should one want to deliberately drown himself, it would be practically impossible to achieve.

And still, somehow, dozens each year are managing it by accident?

Upon closer scrutiny of some of these drownings, a few have recently been upgraded as homicides, either by law enforcement and/or medical examiners. Soon, as more and more parents with lost sons press for answers, and the circumstances of their deaths are revisited, more cases are sure to follow suit. A storm is brewing, therefore, and it's not proper nor prudent for public officials to continue hiding their heads in the sand. They must follow through now—intensely examine the files, and every new death that's added to them, and then share that data with other agencies throughout the Corridor of Death.

Many well-respected criminologists and pathologists have already verified the existence of a victim class in the northland. Further, they've cited a statistical deviation on height and weight as a mere 0.40 which also appears to be similar regarding the victims' age and race.

But there are other commonalities that could be as easily identified in order to establish beyond a doubt that this grouping is not due to freak chance or regional/climate-based factors and coincidence: All the victim profiles should be additionally analyzed to provide statistical data for the following:

1. Are there any drowning anomalies in each victim's recovery? (e.g. refloat date was not consistent with water temperature and the initial date of disappearance/drowning. Alternately, if divers recovered the body from the bottom before it resurfaced on its own, was the corpse in the proper location; was it found in the correct semi-fetal posture, etc.)

2. Does the description and/or the photo of each recovered corpse resemble what it ought to for the number of days the victim was missing/drowned and factoring in the effect water and air temperatures would have had on decomposition within the respective timeframe?

3. Are there any drowning anomalies in each victim's autopsy? (e.g. no water in stomach; the eyes closed tightly or else cloudy if open; presence of foam in an otherwise dry drowning; evidence of antemortem/postmortem injuries when there shouldn't be or else none where there should, etc.)

4. What is the ratio of dry drownings to wet drownings within the victim class? (if normal this figure would be equal to the nationwide drowning statistics of less than 20%)

5. What is the ratio of agonal muscle bruising or ruptures within the victim class? (if normal this figure should be equal to nationwide stats of at least 10% but not greater than 15%)

6. How many victim's cellphones were actually recovered, and in what condition?

7. How many victims reportedly attempted to call someone at or around the moment of their alleged disappearance?

8. How many victims were originally headed in the opposite direction of where they drowned?

9. How many victim's BAC (blood/alcohol) tests were dangerously high (e.g. blackout level) – how many were at a level where it wouldn't have seriously impaired motor skills—including walking, sitting, crouching or standing—for a person of their weight and height?

10. How many victim's BAC readings could be deemed within normal range for putrefaction?

11. How many victim's toxicology tests showed noticeably elevated GBH levels, accounting for putrefaction?

12. How many victim's toxicology tests showed the presence or even trace amounts of other drug substances—either lawful or contraband—in their systems at the time of death?

If any clear patterns can be established from the above inquiry, and I expect that they can, then the critical *who, what, where, when, why* and *how* question drill needs next to be asked. Because of public fears about police involvement, this inquiry should include interrogating officers who were on duty at the time of each disappearance, as well as those who may have been off duty but were near to each crime scene.

If a truly impartial investigation of this nature rules out police misconduct, then these type of questions should be posed by investigators:

1. Who did the victims have in common in their day to day lives?

2. What favorite pastimes did the victims all regularly engage in?

3. Where might the victims have known each other from, other than a bar or a party?

4. When was the last time any of them engaged in an activity out of the norm for them?

5. Why would this particular profile be important to victimize?

6. How are the victims being pre-selected and by whom?

Official denials are not fixing anything; the deaths, and the doubts they generate, still linger. Composing an authoritative and independent database of these fatalities is the best step forward right now in getting to the bottom of the drowning mystery. It's also the first step taken whenever investigative agencies are truly trying to ascertain who a killer or killers may be. At this point, legitimately undertaking to do so would also show a long-overdue measure of good faith.

For years many concerned citizens have been following these neglected cases on their own, diligently tracking and posting area news reports of missing young men (and where their bodies are recovered from) on dedicated websites and blogs. They have been doing this with the vain hope that authorities will one day take notice of the staggering numbers and begin to do the job themselves.

Because there have been so many non-recreational drowning deaths to record, these public lists are already fairly comprehensive and updated constantly, so it wouldn't be that daunting a task for the FBI and similar agencies to begin constructing an official database for the purpose of launching a *complete* investigation this time.

In light of all the evidence, that is certainly not too much to ask, and I pray it will be done.

As to my own conclusions and beliefs, these probably aren't hard to glean, so I'll only offer this in closing: If I had a son in the 17 to 30-year age bracket, who lived anywhere in the Interstate 90 and 94 corridor, I'd urge him to be extremely vigilant whenever he was out and about, especially if with his friends and drinking in the months of September through April.

Because one thing is for sure in all this, if a young man fails to exercise caution these days and he's bright, popular and athletic, there's an ever growing possibility he could simply disappear one night, and end up later in a nearby body of water, drowned.

RESOURCE INDEX
(Links active in all digital editions)

- http://www.house.leg.state.mn.us/sessionweekly/art.asp?ls_year=86&issueid_=43&storyid=1297&year_=2009 Brandon's Law now expands police priority searches to include missing & endangered adults

- http://www.dundee.ac.uk/forensicmedicine/notes/water.pdf drowning analysis, University of Dundee

- http://lifeloom.com/II11Aggrawal.htm drowning forensics primer

- http://www.cdc.gov/nchs/data/hus/hus10.pdf CDC's 2010 Death & Dying statistics

- http://en.wikipedia.org/wiki/Ted_Bundy serial killer profile

- http://www.fbi.gov/stats-services/publications/serial-murder symposium results

- http://en.wikipedia.org/wiki/Jack_the_Ripper serial killer profile

- http://www.missionhospitals.org/top10causesofdeathinmen statistics

- http://www.npr.org/templates/story/story.php?storyId=7608386 Dying in Police Custody: "Excited Delirium" Legit Diagnosis or Police Cover up? – NPR article 2007

- http://www.ncbi.nlm.nih.gov/pubmed/12850077 making accurate BAC calculations in drownings

- http://www.modernmedicine.com/modernmedicine/Modern+Medicine+Now/Taser-Injuries-Require-Preparation-in-ERs/ArticleNewsFeed/Article/detail/532185?searchString=Taser Injuries Require Preparation In ERs hospitals now preparing for more taser injuries & death

- http://www.allgov.com/Controversies/ViewNews/90_Percent_of_Taser_Death_Victims_are_Unarmed_120318 90% of police taser victims are unarmed – article 2012

- http://www.sj-r.com/top-stories/x1089263676/Police-Tasers-safe-effective US Dept of Justice says tasers not safe - 2010 – "Excited Delirium" bogus diagnosis for sudden deaths in police custody

- http://www.homicidecenter.org/Research Brief on Smiley Face Murder Theory - FINAL.pdf Center for Homicide Research's 2010 study "Drowning the Smiley Face Murder Theory"

- http://findarticles.com/p/articles/mi_go1613/is_3_15/ai_n29287772/ American College of Forensic Examiners 2006 report on drowning as murder

- http://staff.lib.msu.edu/harris23/crimjust/serial.htm Michigan State Univ. Criminal Justice Dept brief

- http://en.wikipedia.org/wiki/Rampart_scandal LAPD Rampart Division's CRASH unit scandal

- http://www.usfa.fema.gov/downloads/pdf/publications/tr-141.pdf 2003 FEMA report: "Firefighter Arson"

- http://nationwideinvestigations.us/case1.html detectives Gannon & Duarte

- **Book Recommendation**: **http://www.amazon.com/Studies-Drowning-Forensics-Kevin-Gannon/dp/1439876649/ref=sr_1_1?s=books&ie=UTF8&qid=1333281548&sr=1-1**

- http://www.gwu.edu/~nsarchiv/news/20010306/ U.S. Nat'l Security Archives – Operation Condor

- http://www.geocities.com/~virtualtruth/condor.htm about Operation Condor

- http://surfdete.ipower.com/smileyface.html discussion boards

- http://chicago.cbslocal.com/2011/05/20/2-investigators-are-murder-statistics-being-watered-down/ 2011 article

- **Book Recommendation: http://www.amazon.com/Wheres-Opie-Vanished-Chicago-ebook/dp/B006WKL2VI/ref=sr_1_5_title_1_kin?s=books&ie=UTF8&qid=1333281762&sr=1-5**

- http://news.google.com/newspapers?nid=976&dat=20070913&id=rWQkAAAAIBAJ&sjid=JPkFAAAAIBAJ&pg=1035,23973804 2007 news article "No Smiley serial killer in Wisconsin...")

- http://voices.yahoo.com/is-smiley-face-killer-result-denial-coincidence-2925709.html?cat=17 article

- http://footprintsattheriversedge.blogspot.com/ missing/drowned database & blog

- http://sfkillers.com/ missing/drowned database & blog

- **Book Recommendation: http://www.amazon.com/dp/B003VPWW4I** download "Footprints in Courage" the up close and personal account of the Chris Jenkins murder investigation

- http://en.wikipedia.org/wiki/Columbine_High_School_massacre a timeline & overview

- http://www.pbs.org/weta/thewest/people/a_c/custer.htm profile George Armstrong Custer

- http://www.missingkids.com/missingkids/servlet/PublicHomeServlet?Language Country=en_US Nat'l Center for Missing & Exploited Children
- http://news.google.com/newspapers?nid=1988&dat=20050702&id=wlAiAAAA IBAJ&sjid=Oa0FAAAAIBAJ&pg=6030,282746 archive - body of Todd Geib found in lake
- https://m.facebook.com/profile.php?id=105823769445125&refid=17&_ft_=fbid .181285568655419 join the "Reopen Todd Geib's Case" facebook campaign
- http://boston.cbslocal.com/2010/11/02/drunken-accident-or-murder-mystery/Greg Hart death = "Accident or Murder?"
- http://www.examiner.com/headlines-in-providence/providence-police-under-scrutiny-by-family-of-dead-man-family-offers-20-000-reward-for-information Harts dispute Providence Police version of son's death
- http://www.examiner.com/headlines-in-providence/rhode-island-police-cocaine-ring-more-providence-cop-arrests-likely reward for Greg Hart info upped to $70,000 by family
- http://en.wikipedia.org/wiki/Scream_(film_series) about *Scream* "Ghostface" slasher horror film series

find more works from this author @
http://KillingKillers.blogspot.com

Made in the USA
Middletown, DE
06 March 2017